Tempus ORAL HISTORY *Series*

Warrington
voices

Mr Samuel Woodward, lamplighter, at work outside St Clement's Mission in Lower Bank Street in the 1930s.

Tempus ORAL HISTORY *Series*

Warrington
voices

Compiled by
Janice Hayes

TEMPUS

First published 2000
Copyright © Janice Hayes and Warrington Borough Council, 2000

Tempus Publishing Limited
The Mill, Brimscombe Port,
Stroud, Gloucestershire, GL5 2QG

ISBN 0 7524 1037 7

Typesetting and origination by
Tempus Publishing Limited
Printed in Great Britain by
Midway Clark Printing, Wiltshire

Cover illustration: *Cockhedge Mill dressed to celebrate Armistice Day
at the end of the First World War in November 1918.*

A Fairfield Motors charabanc prepares to leave the corner of Padgate Lane, near Manchester Road.

Contents

Introduction

In 1977 Warrington Museum staged an exhibition of photographs which had been commissioned by Warrington Borough Council to record the changing township of the 1900s. Visitors found they could identify with their ancestors as they too were witnessing the disappearance of familiar landmarks as the new town centre began to take shape. Several people tentatively remarked, 'I've got some old photographs at home, but I don't suppose you'd be interested in those as they're only ordinary family pictures not official events.'

A little later I was confronted at a local community centre by a man who felt the museum had little relevance to ordinary working people. 'In years to come when you tell the story of our recent strike,' he said, 'you'll only tell the official story taken from the local paper and that'll be the bosses' view, not the workers'.'

Both of these incidents were the impetus for *Warrington Voices*. Since then the museum has been actively recording old photographs of family life, school classes, transport, local workplaces, VE Day parties and other events as well as the more common street scenes. These in turn have been the subject of new exhibitions and slide talks, which have provided lots of snippets of information about the photographs. People were only too happy to volunteer the information, particularly if they thought they were telling the museum something new! They felt a sense of pride that their story was recognized as part of the town's history. We were able to throw a new light on some of the objects in the museum's collection and fill in gaps in our knowledge of Warrington's past.

We had also come to realize that what had been preserved in the collections was often inevitably biased towards particular classes of the community. An expensive satin wedding dress would be carefully stored away in an upper middle class wardrobe and survive to be donated by the wearer's grandchild. Meanwhile the everyday dress of a working class housewife was usually worn and washed to destruction and then recycled as a rag, rug or duster. We had boxes of a craftsman's moulding planes but not even a weaver's shuttle from the Cockhedge Mill and still less on local trade union history.

A recently donated sanitary pail may not be lovely to look at or worth a great deal of money but is bound to bring back memories for those who remember Warrington's infamous 'tub toilets'. Many more everyday articles were gone forever. Recording local people's memories was one way of redressing the balance.

The extracts in *Warrington Voices* are mostly drawn from tape-recorded interviews with local people during the twenty years I have been associated with the project. A number have been taken from tapes recorded by volunteers, a few come from written life stories to accompany the photographs which have been loaned for the archive. The words are those of the people themselves, editing has been kept to a minimum. The opinions are those of the interviewees. They are not authorized views but reminiscences and snippets of information. Together they are the pieces of the community's past but as this is an ongoing project some of the pieces are still missing.

Oral history is not an exact science, just as conventional history cannot provide a neat and tidy explanation of the past. Perhaps more than any other generation, we have instant access to information about events as they happen. We hear them exhaustively analyzed by political commentators and see sports action endlessly replayed in slow motion. Yet we are suspicious of the truth of the facts presented to us. We know the political bias of the media moguls, we doubt the statements of the PR men and are convinced that an Arsenal fan would not give an unbiased view of Manchester United's performance! Perhaps we should employ this same caution with accounts of historical events.

Our view of events is also coloured by our individual perspective. A work's manager has a different viewpoint than a shop floor worker while a passionate supporter of the early Labour party has a less rosy opinion of a Tory grandee than one of their employees. Both accounts are valid but we may never know the truth from this distance of time. If enough accounts agree, however, perhaps it really happened that way! For example, when several people of a similar age across the town recalled playing at mugshops, this obviously represented a children's pastime at a given moment in time.

Oral history can also preserve the past at second hand. Children recall tales told to them by their parents or grandparents in vivid detail and, although a little might have been altered in the repetition of the tale, it is often still a valuable piece of indirect evidence. Some events are still almost too painful, like the wartime bombing of the Thames Board fête where those directly involved are still sometimes reluctant to confront their memories.

Conventional wisdom suggests that all oral history interviews should be undertaken in a quiet place between just the interviewer and interviewee. It certainly makes life easier! However, a number of extracts in *Warrington Voices* come from group sessions recorded by local Memories Groups in Community Centres and Day Centres across the town. Stimulated by photographs from the Museum's archives, the participants reminded each other of past events and personalities and contradicted each other to get the story right. Even if this was occasionally not as reliable as conventional methods, memories were jogged – and we all had fun in the process!

Warrington Voices has been compiled to commemorate the 150th birthday of the Museum and Library in 1998. Reporting on the laying of the foundation stone of the present building in 1855, the *Warrington Guardian* remarked, 'Warrington … will have one of the first buildings erected as a People's Museum. Let the people feel that the Museum is theirs.'

I hope that this volume will encourage many more 'ordinary' Warrington people to find a voice and share their personal histories with the rest of the community for the benefit of future generations.

Dutton Street, Howley, celebrates becoming the best-dressed street at King George V's Jubilee in 1935.

Acknowledgements

I would like to thank the numerous individuals and their families who have agreed to record their memories or who have loaned photographs. Several community groups have also contributed to the project; notably the Latchford History Group and the Dallam Memories Group, both organized in conjunction with Priestley College Outreach Team. Thanks also to the Unlock the Past Group, organized with Warrington Collegiate Institute, and also to the members of the Loushers Lane Memories Group.

The memories of Harry Hardman (Ref. GR29) and Mrs Bradley (Ref. GR26 & 27) were recorded by the Warrington Workshop for Voluntary Action and appear courtesy of Warrington Library. John Leslie Hearn's contribution appears courtesy of the Bewsey Old Hall Conservation Project. Thanks also to numerous members of the staff of Warrington Museum and Warrington Library, past and present, and to the *Warrington Guardian*.

The majority of photographs have come from family albums and others from the official archives. Every effort has been made to trace the copyright holders and to acknowledge the contribution the photographers have made to preserving the Community's history.

Janice Hayes

CHAPTER 1
Childhood

Three-year-old David Plinston poses with his toy car outside his house in 1926.

The Pedal Car

A child's pedal car, vintage 1926, standing outside a small terraced house, in a street of small terraced houses. This is my earliest memory. I was three years old at the time and was photographed in the car. In those days the Sunday newspapers like *The People* and *The News of the World* would enlarge your favourite snap very cheaply, and obviously my parents took advantage of the offer.

David Plinston

Childhood playmates in the early twentieth century.

Games and Toys in the 1920s

We'd play lots of different games: rounders, hopscotch, maybe cricket, shuttlecock and bat, skipping with lots of little jingles and Kick Can Lurky. Occasionally one of the boys would play, but if they didn't want to play with the girls we wouldn't have minded.

We liked skipping best. It depended on the rope how many of us went in, whether we had a long rope or a shorter rope. We sang:

> 'Queen, Queen Caroline,
> Dipped her hair in turpentine,
> Turpentine made it shine,
> Queen, Queen Caroline'

and then you all ran out. Then you ran in and said:

> I saw Esau, sitting on a seesaw,
> Shouting, shot, bullet, fire!'

and then you ran out. If you got your legs caught up in the rope you had to turn the rope. I think that was our favourite game on cold days.

We played hopscotch and throwing the ball to one another, but that came in with the rounders. Then somebody got a net and we had a go at netball. If the ball was in somebody's backyard you'd got to wait until you got it back. We played mostly in the street but there wasn't a lot of traffic then. We tended to play mostly in front of the house unless we went to the park which was nearly half a mile away, but it was quite safe in those days.

I got a book every Christmas and when we were going to school we'd call in the library at the local post office. My word, she'd have a look at your hands before she'd let you have a book to make sure they were clean. We had board games, ludo, tiddlywinks and card games.

I got nine old pence pocket money, sixpence for the bank and threepence to spend. I didn't spend it all because I used to save two pence to buy little presents for my mother and father. I spent the penny because all the other children only had a penny pocket money. I got the money on a Friday night. I usually got birthday presents and I used to get a card from my school friend because they'd only just come out in those days. There weren't a lot of cards about but they were the single, shiny cards.

Phyllis Pickering

Childhood Crazes

I remember that we used to have seasons, I mean periods of time, when it seemed that everyone would have a craze for one or other pastime. For example, the boys would play faggies, a game with many variations. Basically the players would hold a cigarette card between two fingers and then with a quick flick of the wrist flirt it against a wall. You would usually be knelt down facing the wall and the winner would be the one who could pitch his card so that it touched any other card already on the floor. He was then entitled to claim all the cards. In those days cigarette cards were greatly prized and we went to great lengths to obtain a complete set. It was usual for there to be one card in every pack of cigarettes. Different brands of course gave different cards and collecting these could be an absorbing hobby.

Marbles, or stonies as we called them, was also a popular game. Here again there were many variations: big ring, little ring, killer, nug hole, bobbin' on and many more. Our marbles were initially made from hard baked clay but around 1930 the glass marbles, or glasses as we called them, began to be popular. The basic skill in marbles, apart from having a good aim, is the ability of the knuckler to hit the marble he's aiming at with his own marble – called a tor – without rebounding too far from the rest of the marbles. You had to apply bottom spin, much like playing snooker. Obviously we had our favourite tors and set great store by them. Many is the time I've had my already sore knuckles rapped by the teacher for putting my grubby hands on my books. My hands had got bloody at times through playing nug hole on my way to school, usually because of the rough ground we had to play on.

Kite flying was always good for a week or so. We used to make our own kites, all shapes and sizes. To the uninitiated a slipped bally band or short tailing would not mean much, but to the expert it meant the difference between a successful mission or a total flop. Once we'd got the kite in full flight we could send a message up it. This was a carefully cut piece of paper which was then threaded onto your twine and if you'd applied it skilfully it would gradually ascend up to your kite. I must admit though that this kite flying was sometimes frustrating, especially if there was no wind. As we didn't have enough ground to get a good run up to get the kite off the ground one of our pals would sometimes throw the kite up for you. They were never keen to do this because if it flopped they were always to blame.

Then there were tops: tops of all shapes and sizes which were sent merrily on their way, sometimes through windows, and usually as a threat to life and limb! We had whip tops, which were similar to a mushroom and had a steel spinning tip which was flush to the wooden stem. You spun these with the tips of the fingers of both hands and as they revolved you hit them frantically with a thick piece of string on a stick to make them go faster.

This form of spinning top was looked on as rather effeminate or childish and all the big lads aged over ten were exponents of the peg top or 'peggies'. These were more round in shape and squat with a longer steel point as a spinning tip. A length of cord was wrapped tightly and neatly round the body of the top, with the end of the cord looped and fastened to your finger. The success or failure of the exercise depended how proficient you were when you flung out your arm and with a spin of your wrist, sent the top spinning away. A hard-topped surface was required for this pastime and usually the school playground was ideal, but you can imagine that the

A portrait of the Day family: father Lionel ('Lion'), mother Emily, Ernie aged eight (centre) and younger brother Jack.

rate of injuries made this venue out of bounds. The only suitable place was Thewlis Street as this was the only street in the area that had been overlaid with tarmac, all the remainder were cobbled with pavements. Consequently Thewlis Street was a recreational area which we called the New Road. Seeing it now it's difficult to imagine children playing on it but you have to remember that the amount of traffic using it in those days was negligible, especially after the traders' vehicles had finished for the day.

Jacks was another favourite game played by all ages, both indoors and out of doors. Girls as well as boys enjoyed the game. The five jacks were made of heavy glazed clay, brightly coloured and about an inch cube in size and shape. The players sat grouped around on the floor and the jacks were tossed off the palm of the hand onto the floor in a sequence of progressively more difficult moves. Ones, twos, threes, fours, fives, cracks, no cracks, dog kennels, finger ends and flights were all variations on throwing up the jacks whilst performing dextrous manoeuvres.

The girls too always seemed to be fully occupied with skipping, hopscotch and various permutations of bouncing the ball. By constant practice some of the girls became expert catchers and ball manipulators. One girl, Vera Scott, who lived at the back of our house in Pickmere Street, was amongst the best. Vera would hold her dress up with one hand so as not to impede the ball and with the other perform wonderful slight of hand tricks such as keeping a ball bouncing under and over her legs against a wall. This had to be seen to be believed!

None of us had bikes and in fact it was not until you started work that you could afford this ultimate luxury. Everywhere we went we trotted and walked, depending on the urgency of the journey. One activity which helped in this respect was called trundling. A trundle was a hoop about thirty inches in diameter, made of either wood or steel, and controlled by a hook which you held in your hand to roll the hoop along as you ran. My dad was a wiredrawer and made my brother Jack and I a trundle each out of a continuous loop of wire rope. They didn't bounce as much as a steel one and lasted much longer than wood. These made us the envy of all our mates and lightened many an errand to the shops on The Green.

Ernie Day

Childhood Games

When we were very young we didn't have radio or TV only an old gramophone. If we got bored playing ludo or snakes and ladders we would go across the road to the shops and play guessing games on goods in the windows. Sometimes we would buy a very small halfpenny doll and line a matchbox to make a little box for it. We could then dress the doll and carry it round in a pocket. We did the same with larger dolls and put them in shoeboxes, put a tape through the box and pulled it along the street.

Mayor Peter Peacock presents toys to Warrington children during the First World War.

Collecting home-made toys for local children during the Second World War.

A good game for both boys and girls was to tie string through holes punched in the tops of two empty soup cans and use the cans as miniature stilts for walking on. There were dozens of games to play in the street; top and whip, hopscotch, marbles or 'cullies', fag cards, skipping, mug shops, trundles and diabalo. I loved to play with a large handbag filled with empty scent bottles, powder boxes and scrap cards for rent books and club books, pretending to be grown up. Another pastime was to ask mums if we could take their baby for a walk. Of course we would only go to houses where the mothers gave the biggest pieces of chocolate.

There was also a rather strange game of visiting the dead. If anyone died in the surrounding streets it was quite in order to tap on the door and ask if we could see the body. The answer always was, 'Come in,

behave yourself, the body's in the parlour.' We would go in and solemnly view the body, always with the greatest reverence and completely without fear or squeamishness.

Lillian Whitfield

Street Games

Lowerum, which was really an abbreviation of 'lower your bum', was a game played by all ages and both sexes. The participants split into two equal teams and tossed up to see who went first. The losing team lined up with one member of the team, usually the fattest, standing with his back to the wall. The remaining members of his team all crouched, each behind the other, thus making a continuous row of backs. The jumping team then had to vault in turn so as to allow all their side to be on the backs of the opposition, with feet off the floor. If those underneath them collapsed, then the jumpers had another go. If one of the jumpers fell off or failed to get on then the whole process was reversed.

Another game usually played in the dark nights of winter was Kick Can Lurky. A den would be marked out for this, probably against a wall. An area of roughly ten feet by six feet was scratched on the ground. An old tin can was then placed in the centre of the den and one player was drawn to be 'on' by tossing up or some other means. He then had to stay in the den until the remainder had scattered and hidden.

The person who was on then had to seek out the people who had hidden and bring them back to his den. They were kept there until one enterprising person who hadn't been caught was able to lure the den keeper away from his lair, run through the den and give the can an almighty kick on the way. This released the prisoners from captivity. As the can was kicked away the cry rang out, 'Kick Can Lurky!'

If the keeper was able to catch all the players without his den being breached then he had won and the game was restarted by choosing someone else to be on. Other variations on this game were Leevo and Tic Tac.

Ernie Day

Playing out was thirsty work for Ernie Day, aged eleven, and his brother Jack.

Playing Shops and Camping Out

We used to go near the old Borough General Hospital where there was lovely brown clay in the earth and get a big lump of it. Then we sat on our back steps making model cakes with coloured buttons and bits of all sorts on. Boiled ham would be a big cob of clay with a piece of wood stuck in it and we'd cut it to serve a quarter. The scales were the best things out, just a piece of wood with a piece of coal on it. We'd measure things on these scales and then wrap them up in newspaper. Then we'd play mug shops. We'd collect pieces of glass and mug, like bits of a china cup that had lovely little flowers on. You used to pray that somebody broke something! Then you'd put it in these empty cocoa tins, just like in a shop. Or there were bits of coloured glass, but I'd never sell my red and green glass – ever. If somebody bought it you'd go and buy it back with a button.

We had a tent made out of a spud bag cut up the middle. They stank those spud bags did and the tent would be nailed on your back wall next to the tub lavatory! We'd sit in that smelly tent and ask our mothers to bring our dinners out and that was usually a jam butty. They'd say, 'You're not having anything to eat near to that closet', but we'd sit there until they brought it out. You could buy a little stove then from Woolies [Woolworth's] for a tanner. It had two little holes in the top for two little pans and you put a night light underneath. We used to melt dolly mixtures in the pans and it made a horrible stink and the pan handles would be red hot. But we had a whale of a time!

Lillian Whitfield

Buttercupping in the 1940s

Where Greenalls' later buildings were in Loushers Lane, there were three tremendously

Taylor's bookstall in the old Warrington General Market.

Reading quietly at Warrington Library, 1930s.

deep wells and it was a marvellous field for buttercupping in and things like that. The wells were marvellous for going frogspawning and worrying your mother sick! We used to go to the Dingle at Appleton. We'd take some pop and sandwiches wrapped in greaseproof paper. The thought of a child going to the Dingle on their own now!

Wendy Wiles

Pocket Money

Depending on our age we had between a farthing and a penny a week. We had to do jobs to get our pocket money, like taking jam jars or beer bottles back to the shop. We had to stone the back step, run errands and darn socks. Some of us had to write out bets, clean shoes or collect pensions.

We spent our pocket money on sweets like ducks, potatoes and peas – which were like wine gums, stick jaw, cinder toffee, liquorice root, gobstoppers, lollipops, dolly mixtures, sherbet dabs, aniseed balls, jelly babies, tabaco which was coconut rolled in cocoa and double six sweet bars.

Mosslands Memories Group

17

Rover and Biggles

On Saturday nights I would go as late as possible to Taylor's bookstall in the market. Providing they were clean and not too creased they would let me swap my copies of *Rover*, *Wizard* and *Hotspur* for an equivalent number of second-hand comics which they had for sale. I always thought that was very kind of them.

When I was a little older I used to visit the children's section of the public library, usually on my way home from school at four o'clock. The lady in charge was fearsome indeed, with cropped hair and rimless glasses. We would walk to her desk at the entrance and she would say one word, 'Hands!' Then we held out our hands for her to look at. There were always one or two people turned away because their hands were not clean enough. Usually we would go outside, spit on our hands, wipe them on our trousers and go back inside. We were never refused entry on the second occasion, but always told to wash our hands properly the next time.

Once inside the library you would try to find a Biggles story but these were very popular and sometimes difficult to find. As far as I was concerned the William stories of Richmal Crompton were a very good alternative. The escapades of William, Ginger and the gang were always good for a laugh and on many an evening at home I have laughed until the tears came, while the rest of the family wondered what was causing the uproar! I don't think we had a radio in those days so most of our spare time, in the winter at least, was taken up with reading and talking.

David Plinston

The End of Childhood

I was born in 1918 and I remember the General Strike of 1926. My Uncle Bob had made me a wooden fort out of a tea chest and I treasured it a great deal. At the time we had no coal, in fact we had been without for weeks, either because of the Strike, which was of course the total withdrawal of all industrial labour in Britain, or because my Mam and Dad just didn't have the money. The stark fact was that anything that would burn was used as fuel and things were so desperate that even our furniture was in jeopardy. I came downstairs one morning to go to school to find Mam in our little kitchen putting the remains of my beloved fort under the boiler for the weekly wash. When she saw me she burst into tears and hugged me to her, telling me through her tears how sorry she was. I think I grew up a little during those few minutes.

Ernie Day

Growing Up

Even though we started work at fourteen we were still kids. I started work with my hair in two plaits! You were twenty-one when you sort of got to do what you wanted. You might have got the key of the door but if your parents said that you had to be in for ten o'clock, then ten o'clock it had to be – not two minutes after it.

Margaret Barlow

CHAPTER 2

Home and Neighbours

Edith Warburton (the author's grandmother) poses outside 28 Dalton Bank. Despite being an unofficial nurse and midwife to the neighbours, she was unable to save baby Stanley from an outbreak of scarlet fever.

Family Life in the 1920s and '30s

I was born at home at number 74 Cartwright Street, Bank Quay, on 24th November 1922. I was the eldest of four children. My mother had come to Warrington at the age of eleven from the Cardiff area of South Wales. She came alone, in the charge of the guard on the train to take up work in service. The rest of her family soon followed because jobs were hard to find in South Wales.

My childhood home was a two-up and two-down terraced house. The only heating was a coal fire in the living room. The toilet, which was down the backyard near the gate, had a wooden seat with an open tub underneath it. Every Monday a cart came

An infant Lillian Whitfield with her parents Albert and Georgina Best.

round and emptied all the tubs. My mother worked very hard keeping everything clean and free from vermin.

It was a day's work doing the weekly wash because everything was scrubbed and boiled. We had to dry everything in the living room if the weather was bad. A very large rack was lowered from the ceiling, filled with washing and then raised to the ceiling over the fire to dry. This made the living room very damp and cold in winter.

In winter my dad used to take a hot shelf out of the oven, wrap it in very thick brown paper and put it in our beds to warm them through. He also mended our shoes using threepennyworth of leather from the tanning works which was enough to sole

and heel two pairs of shoes. We got into real trouble if we kicked the toes out of our shoes and we were threatened that if we did we would have to go to the police station to get fitted out with clogs. This made us very careful because clogs were a sign of poverty.

Lillian Whitfield

Life in a Terrace, 1930s-1950s

As a child I lived with my brother and parents, John and Anne MacDonald, in a two-up, three-down terrace house at 109 Cumberland Street, Latchford. There was no bathroom, the toilet consisting of a pail closet in the back yard. Each week it was emptied by men dressed in khaki coloured overalls, rubber boots and rubber aprons. The smell was overpowering and yet my mother and thousands like her took pride in scouring the wooden seat of that pail closet. Over the years of course a water closet became the norm but it was still in the backyard and so chamber pots in the bedroom were a boon, particularly on a cold night! We bathed weekly in a tin bath in front of the fire. In about 1950 a modern bathroom was built over what was called the 'back kitchen'.

The front room of the house was the best room, called the parlour. It was only used for visitors at Christmas and for doing our homework in. The middle room was the main living room, containing a coal fire in a black leaded range. Gradually this too was modernized into a tile-surrounded grate containing a smokeless fuel fire with background central heating. The front and middle room were converted into one large living/dining room sometime after I married and moved out.

I had a happy childhood but looking back

I suppose we had it rough. Father was a labourer as most men of the working class were then. Mother didn't work outside the home but as she had few labour-saving devices she had to scour the floors, while washing took a full day and ironing another. Every day had its allotted task. Sitting in my modern central-heated house with fitted carpets, fully equipped kitchen and bathroom and a car in the garage I wonder how we managed then!

Audrey Lewis

Family Life in the 1940s and '50s

The kitchen was dominated by a square table. All our main meals were taken here, but try as I might I can never remember mam having one. She cooked and served but never seemed to eat. Saturday tea always ended with bought cream cakes and we longed for dad to say, as he occasionally did, that he didn't want his. That was a real treat.

Food was carefully rationed and we were forbidden to eat anything without permission. None of the children dared to help themselves to a scone or biscuit or a drink of pop purchased every Monday from Blackburne's delivery lorry at five [old] pence a bottle.

In the main the evenings would be spent playing out but when the weather was changeable and there was none of the regular radio programmes on times could get difficult for children. Mam and dad didn't seem to have a problem. Mam was invariably busy sewing, knitting or rug making and dad had the capacity to while away the hours just sitting in his armchair. Dad worked shifts all his working life as a

Mrs McDonald and daughter Audrey (later Audrey Lewis).

wire drawer at Whitecross Steel Works so, apart from the early six to two shift, evenings were interrupted. After the two to ten shift he would call in the Lower Angel for that last pint, so when he arrived home we were long in bed. He hated that shift.

When he was on nights Mam started preparing his tea can and sandwiches about 8.30 p.m. while dad put on his overalls, cap and scarf and fastened the leather laces of his clogs by putting his feet on the dining chair – an image indelibly printed on my mind. Only when he was on the six to two shift was dad home all evening and I often relieved my boredom by regularly combing his hair and drawing pictures in chalk on the soles of his shoes while he lounged in the armchair.

When Mam was rugmaking we helped by

cutting up old trousers and skirts but more often draped the rug as a tent and crouched underneath it. In the same way the large Singer sewing machine became our stagecoach and dining chairs placed on their backs turned into a two-seater wagon or car. It must have been pandemonium!

Though we made good use of household items to play, I wouldn't want to give the impression that we had no proper toys or games. I had a wonderful Meccano set, dozens of books and lots of board games which were used on Sunday afternoons when a friend or neighbour was invited in. I used to love this. A dartboard hung on the door of the airing cupboard in the back bedroom and dad regularly joined us to play.

As the years went by I became very proud of my parents. They unselfishly provided all

four children with their every need. They worked very hard for little monetary reward but lived their life with great dignity. They never went to church but practiced a truly Christian way of life. They epitomized to me my ideal of working class people.

Ray Brookes

Post-War Married Life

I married in 1956 after my fiancé had served the compulsory two years of National Service in the army; the Royal Engineers and Mechanical Engineers or REME. After our honeymoon in the Isle of Man, like many other young couples then, we lived with his parents. I carried on working, the idea being that we would have a baby after we'd bought our own home. In fact we chose to have a child first as we were so comfortable with my husband's parents. Then we bought a car and four years after our marriage we bought a bungalow which we've extended over the years into a larger house.

Of course I carried on working, not least because I had excellent childcare from my mother-in-law but also because I enjoyed being outside the home and advancing my career. Some called it a selfish attitude but I was encouraged by my husband and in-laws, who enjoyed childcare, to continue to work so that we could have a comfortable home, holidays, television and a car. My husband and I shared household duties with help from my mother-in-law.

So the years went by and I was living a comfortable life when disaster struck in the form of technology or the microchip, computers and word processors. My husband and I suddenly found ourselves in a very

Audrey Lewis' wedding day in 1956.

uncertain world without the industries we'd taken for granted for so long. Engineers like my husband were no longer required and the wide employment opportunities like the wire, steel, paper and cotton industries which Warrington had enjoyed for so long were suddenly gone. You had to adapt and my husband managed to find employment in the public sector in Social Services, looking after slow learners and helping them to obtain jobs requiring merely basic skills. He was lucky that he thoroughly enjoyed this change in his career until he retired at the age of sixty-five.

Audrey Lewis

The Kitchen Fire

The living room, or the kitchen as we called it, had the fire as the focal point. The fireplace was a magnificent cast-iron range which my mother had chromium plated at Richmonds Gas Stove Company. It was quite beautiful and would cost a fortune at today's prices. It consisted of a raised fire basket which burned just about every solid fuel. A deep hob housed the teapot and a cast grill swung over the fire to take pans. I cannot recollect that my mother ever cooked on the fire since there was a gas stove in the back kitchen. The range was used for making toast and roasting chestnuts, and the large oven for baked potatoes, particularly on a Saturday night when mam and dad went to the Labour Club for a drink.

The grate was topped by an elaborately carved cornice. On top of that stood a chiming clock between two brass candlesticks, all beyond my reach. A length of wire was stretched underneath and this was invariably draped with drying clothes. Suspended from the ceiling was the clothes

A rare interior view of a gaslit terraced house in the early 1900s. Eunice Bate also kept a greengrocer's shop at her home at 722 Knutsford Road.

airer, each wooden slat bearing the weight of blankets, sheets, pillow cases and every conceivable item of clothing.

Keeping such a fireplace cleared of ash in the morning and regularly black leading it proved too much for my mam and she followed many others by having it replaced with a nasty ceramic tile grate.

Ray Brookes

Keeping Warm

The oven used to be full of bricks all day: that was for your hot water bottle. It's a wonder the beds didn't catch fire! We all went to bed with a brick. You didn't have as much bedding then, I can remember having overcoats on the bed.

Then there was thermogene. They used to put those thermogene jackets on and they stopped on all winter until they fell apart!

Margaret Barlow

Before Central Heating

Winter mornings posed problems. The house was not heated and Mam never had time before school to prepare the fire. At some stage though we acquired a small electric fire and I huddled in front of it, still dithering with the cold while eating my corn flakes. After this I hated going into the cold bathroom to get ready for school. Mam would always boil a kettle of hot water to make things a little more comfortable.

Ray Brookes

Peg Rugs

You didn't throw anything away, it was cut up for a peg rug. They were very pretty. They were strips of cloth that you pushed through something like hessian. All the family had a go at it.

Phyllis Pickering

The Backs

Working Men's Mission Chapel and Schoolroom in Thewlis Street were just at the back of our house. You had to cross a narrow cobbled passageway which was called The Backs. This linked all the house yards together at the rear and served as a venue for football and cricket matches, bonfires, slanging matches, gossip and gambling schools. It was also for hanging out the washing and this had to be taken in very quickly when the coalman came and the tub carts called to empty the toilets. Yes, The Backs were our playground and our social centre.

Ernie Day

Wash Day Blues

You had a boiler where you had to light the fire underneath. You had to get up at five o'clock in the morning to light the fire and it was six o'clock at night before you'd finished. You did all the washing in that one lot of water. You started with the whites and then the colours and then down until you got to father's overalls. Can you imagine the colour of the water by the time you'd finished? You couldn't change the water because you couldn't afford the time it took to boil clean water. The boiler used to have a wooden top on it for when you'd finished and on Sundays there'd be a cake on there or maybe an apple pie.

Mary Aldred

Doing the Washing

Luckily, washing didn't have to be done in the back kitchen but in a lean-to shed which dad had built before I was born. It was fitted with a gas point and a round gas boiler made of galvanized steel with a copper bottom. Clothes were boiled in this and then

Drying the washing in the backyard of 38 Battersby Lane in the 1950s.

transferred to a dolly tub where they were rinsed. From the dolly tub they were fed through an enormous mangle and folded before hanging to dry. A dry day must have been a real blessing. Stained collars and cuffs were first treated by rubbing a block of green soap over them and scrubbed over the rubbing board which was always propped up in the corner with the posser.

Ray Brookes

Mangling and Ironing

Our mangle, which was the object of many an hour's fun, was a huge cast-iron, framed monstrosity about six feet high. It had two sycamore rollers which were moved by a cogged gearwheel and turned by a large handwheel. The space between the rollers could be adjusted by a spring-loaded wheel on top. The mangle was kept in our shed, which was like a timber lean-to and was in

Washday with dolly peg, dolly tub and mangle in the days before fitted kitchens.

fact later turned into a kind of kitchen.

When we were very young this wonderful contraption served us as a ship, a submarine, a tank, in fact all sorts of things. We could climb onto it and by turning the wheels our imagination ran riot. Incidentally, there were not many people who at one time or another didn't get their fingers under the rollers.

The clothes were then pegged out on the clothes line, either in the yard, or if there were lots of sheets, the line would extend into The Backs. That took up most of the day, together with cooking the meals and other things and the ironing was usually done the following day.

The ironing was done with a flat iron which was heated on the open fire. Possibly two irons were used, one being used while the other was reheated. Of course, these first had to be rubbed clean with either a piece of cloth or emery paper to get off the dirt from the fire. Quite a lot of the garments in those days were heavily starched to stiffen the material. They were either coarse and heavy or lacy and beribboned.

Next was the airing of the newly laundered washing and woe betide anyone who put on a clean shirt or singlet without it first being aired! Normally this operation of airing was done on 'maidens', which these days we call clothes airers. These were simple wooden frames with laths across horizontally for the folded clothes to hang over. The whole frame was duplicated or even triplicated so that it could stand or fold away as required.

We also had a rack which had a complicated pulley rope system. The clothes were draped on the rack at floor level and then the whole thing was pulled up to the ceiling. This idea was always an embarrassment as you grew older and taller because sometimes the garments on the rack had legs and arms so that you had to duck underneath them.

As the house was small and each room upstairs and down was connected by the stairs you could always tell that it was laundry day as you lay in bed by the smell of the soap and the fresh laundry. It was really very pleasant.

Ernie Day

Dreaded Tuesday

Dreaded Tuesday was the day when the Corporation muck cart would visit the area.

In the foreground Emily Day takes a break from washday in the backyard of 56 Lancaster Street.

We didn't have flush toilets in those days and the toilets were sited at the end of the backyard. There was a wooden flap-door in the back alleyway which lifted up so that the men could drag out the tub, which was often full to overflowing. You could always tell when the cart had visited your area as the blue haze and the stench would linger for hours later.

There was no *Top of the Pops* in those days so we would compose our own simple ditties like:

'The Corporation muck cart
was full up to the brim,
Pity help the driver,
he fell in and couldn't swim!'

There was very little hygiene in those days. Wartime soap was produced in a long hard block which was cut to short lengths by the shopkeeper. The corners of the soap were so sharp and hard that we would almost finish up with bruised flesh. The first one to use the soap would have the roughest wash. We had no baths or showers in those days only a portable tin bath tub that we filled from the kettle.

Stan Evans

Hygiene

There was a lot of diphtheria, scarlet fever and TB. Whole families were wiped out with tuberculosis. The family next door to us had it and only one survived out of seven. There was always the fever van in the street. It was a cab with blacked out windows and a nurse would come with a big red cloak on and carry them out to the Isolation Hospital. I remember a very big outbreak of smallpox and my dad had it.

The hygiene was terrible. The toilets were all open pails and you had to be cleaning the backs all the time and swilling them. They never used to come round emptying grids. You had to have flycatchers hanging down to catch the flies. There was no fridges and my dad made a sort of meat safe covered with fine mesh to keep the flies out. Everything had to be covered up; your milk and your sugar had little crocheted things with beads on to keep the flies off.

Then there were the bugs. When you moved into a new house the van was fumigated. Everything had to be scrubbed

The night soil men prepare to empty the sanitary pails they have just exchanged on their rounds of the 'tub toilets' in the late 1950s.

and me and my mother was everlastingly cleaning. We used to get insect powder for the bugs but we had old iron beds with straw mattresses. You had to dust around where the slots were and knock the bugs off. Every week the beds were taken apart and cleaned, otherwise you'd have been overrun.

Mrs Bradley

Keeping Clean

Our mothers used to comb our hair with paraffin for nits and we had open fires! Or sometimes she used a Derbac comb. On bath night we all used to be in this bath in front of the fire and we all used to go in, one after the other. The youngest went in first and then the next. You had to put the boiler on in the back kitchen to get water for the bath. I had three brothers so I had to go in with the lads, but when I was eleven you had to keep yourself away from the lads then.

Margaret Barlow

House-Proud

I remember in 1950 a salesman from the National Cleaner Company knocking on the front door. He persuaded Mam to have a demonstration. My house-proud mother was appalled by the heap of dust he poured onto a sheet of paper after a quick hoover over the rugs. I'm sure my mother would have paid for the rest of her days rather than have the ignominy of a dirty house.

Ray Brookes

A Shortage of Beds

I've slept head to tail with my brother in the Fever Hospital in Aikin Street. That was in the summer of 1936 or '37, about July or August. I remember there was a noise outside and being told that it was a cricket in the grid. My father had pneumonia first and then my youngest brother who was only two finished up in hospital with it too. My eldest brother had diphtheria and then I caught it. He was on his deathbed in the isolation ward and it was touch and go. Then he got a little bit better and as there were so many people ill with diphtheria there was a shortage of beds. That's why he had to top and tail

Tom Harris as a boy.

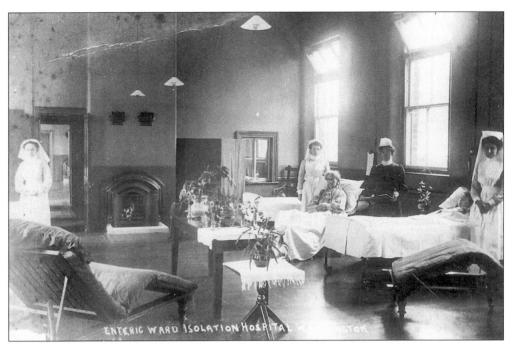

The isolation ward at Aitkin Street Fever Hospital.

with me.

I remember my mother saying that they came from the Borough to fumigate the house and they all had white overalls and masks on. There was nobody cleaner than my mother and our house was spotless, but it was an epidemic.

Tom Harris

The Unofficial Nurse and Midwife

Everybody was always knocking on the door for my mother when someone was ill, when they died or if they were having babies. My mother would say, 'You'd better have the doctor in the morning, I think he's got pneumonia.' She was always on call. She made linseed poultices for

their chests and lungs and she'd nurse them.

If they were having babies they'd run for my mother and she'd stop with them. Then she'd say, 'You'd better get the midwife now.' That was a little old woman called Shelley who lived in Bluecoat Street. Mother would deliver the baby if the midwife hadn't come in time but she wouldn't cut the cord. When somebody had a baby the neighbours would all help out. The midwife would come for so many days but the neighbours would come at eight o'clock in the morning with breakfast. All the neighbours were willing to help each other.

Lots of children used to have fits and they'd come flying for my mother. She'd get mustard between a handkerchief and put it on the nape of the neck. They'd come out of their fit immediately almost.

She saved lots of children's lives. She was like an unofficial nurse and midwife.

Mrs Bradley

Good Neighbours

John Churm lived almost opposite to us at Number 59 Lancaster Street. He had an older brother called Bert, a younger brother Sam who was a friend of my brother Jack, and two sisters, Ina and Nancy. I will never forget the day when Jack and I were playing in our yard and my mother suddenly came to tell John to go home quickly. Then with tears in her eyes she told us that his father had been killed. He was a joiner at Rylands and had fallen from a scaffold.

Mrs Churm was a wonderful woman and was a sort of nursemaid to the whole community. In those days every district seemed to have one, someone to call when any disease or sickness struck. Her knowledge of remedies and potions was a real God-sent gift. You see the doctor's bills were expensive items and he was only called when all else had failed, and usually when Mrs Churm advised it.

She was always the one who did the laying out when a loved one passed away. She was even the unpaid midwife and very often delivered the baby herself. She was the organizer of any kind of collection, from a wreath to a wedding present. She also drowned unwanted kittens, made herb pop and always brought out a big parkin cake on bonfire night.

A horse-drawn hearse probably belonging to Lowden Wells of Foundry Street.

The undertaker leads a horse-drawn funeral in the early 1930s.

How full every day must have been for a woman like that, especially with a family to fend for on her own. Women like her deserved medals for what they did. They were the kingpins of the whole community.

Ernie Day

Death

If someone died my mother would lay them out. She'd wash them, comb their hair and put a nightie on and sheets. The person was never taken away, they were laid out in their own homes until the day they were buried. They were brought downstairs and they'd have them on two trestles under the window. There were no chapels of rest then. The neighbours came in and paid their respects and consoled the family. If the person died in the Fever Hospital though, they were brought home in a coffin.

We used to pay in a Death Club, like insurance for burials. There was an undertaker called Lowden Wells in Foundry Street. People would pay him so much a week after the burial. If people couldn't pay they were put in a pauper's grave, a communal grave in the cemetery.

Mrs Bradley

CHAPTER 3

Around the Town

Bewsey New Hall was built for Lord Lilford in the 1860s but never occupied by the family. It was largely demolished in the early 1940s.

Old Latchford

I was born in 1918 in Rock Road, Latchford. From my mother's bedroom window you could see Irlam Steel Works: it was all meadows between. I remember the first council houses being built at the corner of Reynolds Street, Griffiths Street, Lower Wash Lane and Westy Lane, now Grange Avenue. I remember all the large houses around Latchford. There was Raddon Court where the Reynolds lived; they owned the tannery in Little Wash Lane. Opposite Reynold's Tannery was Parkinson's Tannery. Mrs Parkinson, a widow who owned it, lived opposite to us. Next in Grange Avenue you had Bowden's Farm with Big Barns Piggery, then fields to what is now the Alla Club. Then it was all meadows for miles, no Kingsway Bridge.

Vera Boden

Rural Latchford in the early 1900s, where Westy Lane met Lower Wash Lane, now Grange Avenue.

Westy Lane

I can recall this scene where Westy Lane met Lower Wash Lane. The trees in the distance were there until the 1930s. They fell one by one and were immediately pounced on and carried off in pieces by the local people when everybody had a coal fire and needed kindling.

The farm on the left gave a distinct air of countryside. An old water pump stood on the cobbles of the yard. When I lived in Rock Road nearby until the late 1950s, the occupants were a Mr Blackshaw and his two sisters. They kept chickens and geese in the farmyard and cows in the field next to the Black Bear Canal. They sold eggs and milk and in the summer delicious yellow ice cream.

I used to go to school down the road on the left, also known as Lower Wash Lane, but known to us as 'The Tan' as it led past the tannery, where men could be seen dipping hides in concrete vats let into the ground. Across from the tannery was an engineering workshop with its smell of hot engine oil. That was a time when the town was full of smells and the whiff of one evokes memories yet.

Ron Wray Davies

Blackberry Picking

Out of the centre of Latchford village you were right in the country for blackberry picking. You'd put them in a can like the men took to work. We used to go to the woods at Grappenhall, near Stanney Lunt

Bridge. There were plenty of blackberries there, or we'd go in the meadows round here. We used to go in gangs.

Phyllis Pickering

Going Skating

Ackers Pit used to freeze over and they used to shine their car headlights to see so they could skate.

Phyllis Pickering

Stuck in a Rut

I remember as a child in the 1930s walking down Bridge Street with my mother and a cyclist tried to overtake one of the trams.

As he positioned himself in front of the tram his bicycle wheels became jammed in the tramlines. Everyone around screamed and only the alertness of the tram driver prevented the man being run over. Tramlines were a real danger to cyclists because their narrow wheels could get stuck.

Stan Evans

Workingmen's Mission

Workingmen's Mission did a tremendous amount of work and Crosfields were behind that: they built it. The mission was more than a chapel. It was another form of entertainment for the kids. They used to organize all sorts of things; on a Saturday night it was the Limelights, where they

This 1900s wintry scene is captioned 'Ackers Pits Latchford', but the area was actually part of Stockton Heath, Cheshire, after the opening of the Manchester Ship Canal in 1894.

used to show still photographs. It went right through from Sunday school, the children, then the youths, the young women's classes, married women's classes and so on. My mother used to get herself all dressed up every Thursday afternoon to go to 'class' as she called it. It was part and parcel of everyday life was the Mission. You had to sign the pledge that you wouldn't drink before you were allowed in.

Ernie Day

The Fire Station

Just a few yards down from Heathside School was the local fire station. In those days the fire alarm was signalled by the ringing of a large bell which hung between two forty foot posts in the station yard. The fire service at the time consisted of a fire chief who lived on the premises and two or three officers. The firemen were on a retained basis, most of them living in the streets surrounding the station. Each had a plate over his front door which said 'Fireman'.

Since we lived just around the corner from the station a number of our neighbours were firemen. If the alarm bell rang when we were at home schoolchildren would rush out into the street. It was quite exciting to see the firemen coming charging out of their houses, struggling with braces and jackets

A Stockton Heath tram waits outside Carter's Café, Bridge Street, near to Market Gate.

The old Queen Street Fire Station (left) and the site of the Potato Market (right), photographed around 1960.

while they were running along the street. Sometimes they would be in carpet slippers, sometimes their bootlaces were flying. All this was so they could get to the station, change into boots, helmets etc. and climb onto the engine before it left. As the engine drove away there would always be two or three men still struggling to dress.

Each time there was a fire there would be an audience – mainly schoolchildren – to see the engine depart. Then everyone would be asking, 'Where's the fire?' If the man left in charge of the station was in a good mood sometimes he would tell us. If it was within a reasonable distance there would be a group of youngsters charging through the streets, waiting to watch the fire brigade in action. Sometimes we were

given the wrong information and would end up searching a neighbourhood for a fire which was at the other end of the town!

David Plinston

Bewsey New Hall

I was born at Keeper's Cottage, Burtonwood, in the 1930s. My father, Earnèst Charles Hearn, was a part-time gamekeeper for Lord Lilford, who owned Bewsey New Hall. Later we moved from Keeper's Cottage into Bewsey New Hall Gardens which was the coach house and stables to the New Hall. We had to pay a lot more rent to Lord Lilford, £140 a year,

Martha Hearn, the mother of John Leslie Hearn, feeds her flock at Bewsey New Hall Gardens within the wartime American Base.

Eric Charles Hearn, and Lil and Ernest Charles Hearn with Spot the dog outside Bewsey New Hall Gardens.

which was a lot of money in those days. We had to rely on the orchard fruit trees and vegetables and flowers to sell to help towards paying the rent. The fruit that was plucked had to be graded into sizes and was sold to Mr Bates in Warrington Market.

Mr Gallagher, the gamekeeper, lived in the servants' quarters of the New Hall. Between Bewsey New Hall and Bewsey New Hall Gardens was a large lily pond. Our back kitchen was the coach house and you could see the large bolts and hinges that would have opened into the courtyard when the coaches were brought out. Our parlour was the saddle room and a doorway leading off this would have taken you into the stables. All the time we lived up at New Hall Gardens we had no water laid on, we still got our water from the pump in the yard. There was no electricity or gas, paraffin lights and candles were what we had to use.

Bewsey New Hall was bigger than the Old Hall. When you went in through the main doors there was a large hall with a big sweeping staircase that came right down into it. The library had two doors which slid into the walls when you opened them and the coat of arms was above the doors. There was big long windows inside to view the garden area outside. From the old photograph I had, you could not see at the rear where the north wing ran and where the wine cellars were.

People at Bewsey thought the Hall was haunted, but my father frightened away anybody who tried to go inside for their own safety because some parts had deteriorated. When a lot of the land was taken up by the Burtonwood Air Base, Lord Lilford only had one gamekeeper, Mr Barklett, and when he retired my father looked after the Hall and tried to keep the GIs and other people out. It was a shame to see the Hall deteriorate. There was no repairs carried out and all the windows were broken in time. All the dead leaves from the trees blew inside and my father said that if anybody got inside through one of the broken windows and dropped cigarettes it could be burnt down. My father saw the Estate Agent, who was Mr Atherton from Manchester, and a decision was made that the Hall, apart from the servants' quarters, would be taken down.

When they were pulling the Hall down I was coming home from school through Site 4 when I noticed that some of the men were running around. The one which looked as if he was in charge shouted to me and asked did we have a phone. I told him no and asked what was wrong. He said that they had pulled a section of the first floor out and did not know at the time that there was still a workman inside. The floor had come down on top of him. I said that I would go to the guardroom on Site 4 and get help and an ambulance if I could. GIs came over and helped to get the injured man out, but on the way to Warrington Infirmary he died. I liked the way the Yanks did things, nothing was too much trouble for them. When that army ambulance came up the field towards the field gate he just drove through at full speed. Farmer Stephenson, who farmed at Bewsey Old Hall Farm, I must say was not very pleased!

John Leslie Hearn

Dallam in the 1950s

There were no old people at first, only young people. This was just after the war. Blokes were coming out of the army, getting married, having kids and being pushed up this area to Dallam. You got points to be given houses. You got a point for each child and you got a point for being in the forces. We were married in 1944 and I was still in the Air Force then. I was demobbed and we were living with my mum until we came to Dallam.

There was no bus to Dallam then. You had the bus that brought you from the town to the bridge at the bottom, but you had to get off there and walk over the bridge. Then they had what they called the Penny Bus because it was only a penny fare. Well you got on the Penny Bus and it brought you from this side of the bridge, where the transport club is now, and it brought you down the bottom of

The newly built Dallam estate in the 1950s before the arrival of television aerials and family cars.

Longshaw Street. That was because the bridge wasn't strong enough to take the bus with passengers on. That went on for some time until they strengthened the bridge and after that the buses could come over, or cars. Not that many cars did come up here because people didn't have cars then.

Bill Ireland

Dallam Shops

The first shop at Harrison Square was a baker's shop, Alan Davies opened that. He used to be chief baker at the bakehouse down in Catherine Street at Bewsey. Next door was a hardware shop, the next was a baby linen shop, Mrs Leigh had it. Next door was a grocer's, then a greengrocer's, Len Chadwick kept that. Next door was Robinson's chip shop. Charlie Robinson, his son played for Warrington. None of those shops closed because of the hooligans, it was when they built the Co-op.

The Dallam Memories Group

CHAPTER 4

Schooldays

Bolton Council School infants pose for a typical school photograph in 1922.

Walking to School

In 1947 I always walked to Bolton Council School with my mother until I was in the juniors when I went with my school friends. We were told not to go the 'hilly way' – the back of the tannery behind Raddon Court. We often did, looking for newts and tadpoles. There were mounds of rubbish tipped from the tannery into the ponds where somehow the newts and tadpoles survived. Sometimes we would go to the tannery where the skins were dipped into pits of liquid. Very often we would leap across these pits despite the really pungent smell. Goodness knows what would have happened if we had fallen into one of these pits!

Calling at the shops for sweets was a rare occasion, partly due to rationing but mainly due to the fact that there was not much money about. We would go to Cinderberry's shop across from the school in Reynolds Street where we would buy Lingofizz tablets or kali powder with a stick of liquorice for dipping.

Ruth Brookes

Bolton Council Nursery School in the early 1940s.

Life in the Nursery in 1944

My earliest memories of Bolton School were of being taken to the nursery by my mam when I was about four years old. The nursery building was just inside the school gates at the Longdin Street entrance. It was a single-storey, grey wooden building with a fence around it to separate it from the school playground. Inside there were hooks where you could hang your coat and small tables and chairs. There were camp beds where we could have an afternoon sleep and if it was fine we would play outside in the big square sandpit. We were looked after by Mrs Clementson and Mrs Forber.

Betty Hayes

Heathside School

At the age of seven we moved to the 'Big School', which in those days was known as

an elementary school. Pupils went there until the age of fourteen, but at the age of eleven they had the opportunity to take the secondary school exam. Success in this would mean staying on until the age of sixteen at either the Warrington Secondary School or the Boteler Grammar School.

Heathside Elementary School was quite a happy place despite its forbidding appearance. It might have been mistaken for a prison for it was a tall grimy building surrounded by a concrete yard and high walls with railings. I remember too that the way to the top floor was by one spiral iron staircase and obviously fire safety was not a consideration in those days for I shudder to think what would have happened if there had been a fire.

The layout of the classrooms was strange too. The building was rectangular in shape with a classroom at each end and a large central room on both floors. This central room could be partitioned but in fact rarely was. It was used as an assembly hall each morning and afterwards by two separate classes back-to-back. This was a ridiculous situation as the boys sitting at the rear of the class could hear what was going on behind. More than once I found the subject behind me more interesting than the one my own teacher was discussing!

The heating system was also a joke. Each classroom had a cast-iron stove fuelled by coke but even when they glowed red these stoves would only heat an area a few feet around. This meant that if you didn't sit on the front row you were cold.

For those using the classrooms nearest the street Friday mornings provided a treat. Promptly at eleven o'clock a barrel organ would roll up and provide ten minutes of popular songs. There was nothing that the teacher could do about it of course except to order everyone to get on with their work. What a hope!

David Plinston

Evelyn Street School

During our childhood my brother and I were fortunate that our parents always saw to it that we were fed and clothed as well as could be expected. Most of our trousers, except our Sunday best, were made by my Mam, whilst our jerseys were hand knitted. Many of the lads of my age at school were poorly clothed. Evelyn Street School was in the heart of Sankey Bridges, one of the poorer districts of Warrington and there were quite a few who came to school barefooted. The Chief Constable of Warrington organized a fund to supply children in need with boots and other things and there were many recipients at the school.

In my day it was a comparatively modern school and was in fact one of the first schools to be equipped with a bath. This was not a swimming bath but a large tiled bath about eight foot square by three foot deep where it was compulsory for us to take a bath about once a week. This rule was a local Education and Health decision and created a lot of anger among some parents who objected to the suggestion that their children needed a bath. However, we always enjoyed a bath session – probably because it meant missing a lesson.

Ernie Day

Special Lessons

Bolton was quite a modern school really to some because they used to come from other schools to the laundry and the cookery and we also had a science room.

Phyllis Pickering

St James's School 1930s to 1940s

It was an old fashioned school. Two of the classrooms were in a very big hall and they were separated by a screen that pulled across with little glass windows at the top. There were two or three little classrooms off that and the cloakroom went back from that. Then you went up another passageway to the kitchen where the dinners were prepared, but I never stayed to school dinners.

There was a photograph of Mr George, who was the headmaster at that time, on one of the walls which also had children's drawings on them and things like that. I can remember that glass partition more than

A laundry lesson at Bolton Junior Girls' School in the mid-1920s.

anything else because I was facing it. The teacher was there on one of those tall desks that they climbed up the steps to. We sat two to a desk. There was a sort of lid which lifted up but there was nothing underneath it, only a shelf and inkwells. If you were very good you could fill the inkwells up. The desks were arranged in four columns with perhaps six or ten desks in each column. They were quite big classes – I think there were about fifty in a class.

At break time we used to get those little bottles of milk with a cardboard top which you pushed your finger through. The teacher had halfpenny bars of chocolate which you could buy for your lunch. We used to play out in the playground at playtime. We had our milk and went for a run round the playground or played skipping, hopscotch, tossing a ball up against the wall and standing on our hands

with our skirts tucked up our knicker legs.

I can remember Miss West because she was a tartar and she gave me the cane. She came down from her desk and said, 'This is going to hurt me more than it hurts you', and slammed me across the hand with the cane. That was just for talking in class.

The headmaster after Mr George was Mr Casson. He was a nice chap and he made you laugh. I remember when we were leaving that school we all had to stand up in front of the class and sing. I sang 'You are my sunshine'.

I passed the Eleven Plus exam. There were problems, like arithmetic, and there were intelligence tests where they show you different things and you have to say what is the next one in the series. I can't remember a lot about it but I know it was a big thing. I did pass it and was quite proud. My dad bought me a new bike because I passed it.

Mr Casson wanted me to go to the High School but I did not want to go because none of my friends were going.

Freda Ford

Memories of Sacred Heart School

My most vivid memories are of a tall forbidding building from the outside. Class I and II were divided by a tall partition and you could hear the noise from the adjoining class. I remember gas lights and stone steps and the dark blinds at the window during the war years. I remember the smell of ink and the terrible scratching sound of chalk on the blackboard. I do remember the infants drinking Horlicks out of cups with nursery rhyme transfers which were hung on hooks in the cloakroom. The windows had criss-cross strips on them, because it was the wartime, to prevent them from shattering.

My most vivid memory is of Miss Flood the headmistress, a large lady who was the boss! I remember fainting in assembly and she smacked me on the legs as if I had fainted deliberately! I had to sit in the porch along with a boy who had also fainted. His face was bright red but mine was as white as a sheet. Children frequently fainted, I think it was bad ventilation.

I remember we were very patriotic and being shown the pink on the maps which represented the British Empire. Empire Days were rather like the Last Night of the Proms with Miss Flood singing in an operatic voice and we all waved our flags.

I remember Miss Richardson who looked very stern, but one winter I realized what a

St James' School around 1920, showing the screen which divided the hall and the classrooms.

humanitarian she was. There was one family who were sent to school with holes in their shoes and looked half-starved. She used to boil milk for them in a big boiler in the cloakroom to warm them up.

Members of Unlock the Past Group from Warrington Collegiate Institute, 1997

Empire Day in the 1920s

All the children went to school dressed in clothes of red, white and blue. We all assembled in the playground and the school piano was brought out. We sang patriotic songs such as 'Bluebells of Scotland', 'Danny Boy', 'God Bless the Prince of Wales', 'Land of Hope and Glory' and 'Rule Britannia'. We also had a maypole which we danced around. As the Union Jack was raised we sang 'God Save the King'.

Phyllis Pickering

Classroom Smells

The classrooms smelled of chalk and the heating pipes always used to smell. Sometimes we brought in stink bombs that smelled of bad eggs. The classrooms smelled of carbolic and blue mottle soap. We wore camphor blocks around our necks and took sulphur tablets to school to have after dinner. They were supposed to clear the blood.

The Mosslands Memory Group

'Polly' Hackett's Class

I remember my last year at Bolton Council Juniors. I was a member of Class 4A which was something to be proud of as it was the top class and I was quite chuffed with that. The downside was that the teacher of 4A was a notorious woman called Polly Hackett – Polly Hackett by the pupils of course not

Britannia and her classmates celebrate Empire Day at Bolton Council School in the 1920s.

by the staff. She had a reputation like a number of teachers at that time of being very, very strict, so as young lads we were quite apprehensive of going into her class.

Polly Hackett was a barrel of a woman with a tremendous kind of physical stature. My memory is that she wasn't like a human being; she was more like a caricature. She had a very large eagle-like nose and a large pair of brown glasses across the top of her face and a kind of rounded stomach.

She sat at a raised desk in the corner of the room and seemed like a metre higher than us. From here she would dictate everything, all the instructions were issued from this desk and when we had finished a particular piece of work we would queue at the desk and she would mark it. If you did particularly well you would get a star, if you did particularly badly you would get a telling off or at worst another dose of the cane.

Days in Polly Hackett's class were very structured. Every single morning after assembly right up until break we were drilled in maths, well arithmetic is a better word as we didn't do geometry or algebra. We were given little exercise books and sat in our double desks. Then hour after hour we worked through the sums, sometimes from the blackboard, sometimes from the book. Often the sums were over a page long and it was drilled into us that we had to get all the columns absolutely straight. If the figures weren't straight in the columns punishment could very easily be the cane, which was used frequently.

Tables were drilled into us like teaching a parrot to talk; we literally sang them every single morning. Sometimes as the whole class would have to stand up and recite a particular table the teacher would throw at us, sometimes just one section would have to do it, then again the two people in the

Ray Brookes as a schoolboy.

front desk would be selected. Occasionally you as an individual would be picked on and because you were nervous and got it wrong you were punished.

After break we did other subjects like English, poetry, history or geography but I don't remember those too well ... all I can remember is this great wad of arithmetic every morning.

Friday afternoon or Friday morning there was a test and that test was marked during that day and then you were put in a rigid order, first to last. You tended to find your place and find that with odd exceptions you used to sit in that same place week in and week out. The lads at the other end of the class were just total strangers and you never got to know them.

Ray Brookes

School Dress in the 1940s and '50s

Girls in the main wore dresses with perhaps a hand-knitted cardigan over during the spring and summer terms. We wore short cotton socks with either sandals or galoshes. During the winter term girls sometimes wore gymslips with a jumper underneath. We wore long grey socks and sturdy shoes.

Boys always wore short pants. They were almost invariably grey and finished just above the knee. They were accompanied with long socks, again grey, which were kept up with elastic garters hidden when the tops of the socks were turned down. Shoes were practical – black, laced and heavy. Most of us wore grey flannel shirts and a pullover and jacket. The smarter ones wore a tie. It wasn't unusual to wear such an outfit until the age of thirteen. Casual clothes as we know them today didn't exist then.

The Latchford History Group

'Nitty Nora'

There were regular visits by the school nurse who we called 'Nitty Nora the Bug Explorer'. She also checked the boys had clean hands and necks. There were regular visits by the school doctor and then the girls had to strip down to their liberty bodices.

The Mosslands Memory Group

Mr Barber's class at Bolton Junior Boys' School in 1945.

Typical school dress at Bolton Junior Girls' School in 1948.

Learning to Write

When we doing joined up writing the teacher demonstrated on the board, first one letter, then joined up. We would be there just copying the thing, page after page, with pencils and then dip in pens. Then there was the first biro in about 1947 or 1948. I can remember the teacher suddenly started marking with a biro. None of us had ever seen or heard of one. They were quite slim ones. Eventually they became quite widespread and I can remember asking my mother for a biro and she bought me one but it was a different one from the teacher's as it was shorter and a bit stubby.

Ray Brookes

A Primary Teacher's View

When I came out of college I was a young teacher of twenty-two and we had as many as fifty in a class or fifty plus. Well, of necessity they had to sit facing the teacher. All schools were the same then; they hadn't changed to working in groups. Really you can still teach children as individuals even if they are sitting in blocks, can't you?

All the time I was at Bolton Council School they still had those desks with the lids that lifted up, with books inside. You sat two at a desk but sometimes we used to move the desks around into little groups.

We always had assembly, then the girls would go into their own classroom. We started out with spellings and vocabulary, working the two together. We had a spelling book or else we did spellings of things that were happening around them. It's not much use knowing how to spell a word if you don't know what it means!

Then we did tables and mental arithmetic; I insisted on things like tables. Then we used to do what we called 'mechanical arithmetic': problems and

Learning to write at Oakwood Avenue School in the 1920s or 1930s.

things like that. After play we'd do some sort of reading and free writing, English exercises and cursive writing. Miss Copeland was a beautiful writer and she used to go round to the different classes and teach them writing. We had proper writing lessons because when they came up from the infants they did printing. A lot of them were eager to start and said, 'can we do real writing?' They really had to be taught to do the shapes. I can remember their reading books, the old Beacon books and Old Lob.

Apart from assembly there were scripture lessons. When I became head I used to take all the religious education. We had an epidiascope and you put pictures on the screen, from the Old Testament and the New Testament. The children used to take it in turn to do the assemblies and make up their own, usually in a morning.

By and large it was maths and English in the morning and history, geography and science, or 'nature studies' as we used to call it, all fitted in. There was art and needlework – Miss George was very keen on that, she had very high standards. She was very strict with that, it was blood, sweat and tears!

They had some kind of games activity each day. We'd no playing fields so we had to play rounders and netball and we had things like climbing frames and those boxes that you could jump over.

Blackboards were very necessary but there was a time when the powers-that-be came round and said, 'Get rid of them, you don't need your blackboards.' Then they changed into open-plan, when they didn't have the doors closed, and I could never have enjoyed that. There's a lot to be said for working in groups but I feel there's always somebody who escapes in a way. They can be working on a table, one that's

not particularly good, and they're just leaving all the work to the rest on the table. There's too much noise nowadays, too much distraction. I suppose people would say that's freedom. I don't think it's freedom I think it's licence more than anything.

I'm probably biased but I think we had a very well-balanced education. It proved it because of the number of girls that have done so well in their lives. We had standards and I feel proud because I keep meeting people and reading about all the old pupils and how well they've done. I know lots of people that have gone into nursing and become doctors, physiotherapists or become teachers or librarians. Your infant and junior schools, that's where it all starts isn't it?

Mrs Bennett

Richard Fairclough School

The happiest days of my life were at Richard Fairclough School. It was a lot more grown up than the junior school. You had a house system where everyone was allocated to a house. You had to go round to different classrooms, like the history classroom. You had to walk very genteelly down the verandas, no running. You circulated more there and it was all girls. We had a uniform: a gymslip with a braid round it and a white blouse.

I was Captain of the House and on your house day you would proudly lead all your house into the assembly hall. The other three houses would be there and parents and governors and the head teacher would all be sitting on the stage, but you were the main person on that day. I was in St

Audrey Lewis (née McDonald) and her brother John in 1942.

Patrick's House and we used to sing songs to do with Ireland and I had to make a speech.

I enjoyed every minute that I was at school but I didn't learn as much as children do nowadays. We just learned the basic lessons: arithmetic, English, history and geography. We didn't go any further than that because we were only at Richard Fairclough for three years. I left there and started to go to night school. They just asked you what job you wanted to do and I said 'office work', and that was it. It was up to you to get a job yourself.

Freda Ford

Grammar School and Night School

My brother and I attended Roman Catholic primary schools, passed what was then called the Eleven Plus examination and went on to grammar school. Girls and boys attended single sex schools in secondary education then and it was considered something of a one-upmanship in the 1940s and '50s to pass such an exam. School uniform was rigid and woe betide any girl who didn't conform to the gymslip, blouse, blazer and hated beret!

It was expected that grammar school pupils would have an academic career but I was never cut out to be a teacher, scientist or politician. I wanted to be a librarian but when I graduated, not too badly in 1950, there were no vacancies in the local library. It would have been unheard of then for me to travel by train to Liverpool or Manchester for a job in their public libraries. My mother had always encouraged me in my schoolwork and although she was disappointed that I didn't want to continue my education further she paid for me to attend night school. Whilst I worked by day as a junior clerk in the local education office, in the evening I learned shorthand and typing. This training was to earn me a good living for the rest of my working life.

Audrey Lewis

CHAPTER 5

Shops

Albert Southern's corner shop in Thelwall Lane.

A Co-op Bread Man

The Co-op offices then were down Cairo Street. That's where I went for my interview with a man called Tommy King who was the General Manager. Then you got the letter sent saying when you could start. I started at fourteen. The system was in those days you had to sign an agreement that when you were sixteen you had to give up your job if there were no vacancies in the stores. The general way of progression was to come off the vans, then go and work as lads in the shop, brushing the fronts and cleaning the windows and all that sort of thing, before you were allowed in the shops and the departments.

I was fourteen when I started at the Co-op as a van lad taking the bread out. In those days nearly everybody you went to you

Ron Mottram delivering bread for the Co-op at Lymm in 1956.

just left the bread and they paid you at weekends. We used to write the customer's cheque number on a brick outside the door. When she came to pay you'd say, 'Well your number is such a thing', and she'd look at you in amazement! How could you remember? But of course it was written on the brick!

I spent most of my time on a motorized bread van with a man named England. We used to go round Penketh and Sankey. One day we did Penketh and the next day we'd do Sankey. There were two lads, me and a lad named Fred Backhouse. You were out until all hours at night. At Christmas time I remember my father came looking for me once. It was gone eleven o'clock at night and I was still working. Of course you didn't get any more money, you still only got your eleven shillings and eight pence. It was all part of the job but the work you did you seemed to enjoy. It was a bit like a social life as well as working. You got to know

everybody and everybody got to know you. At Christmas time we did very well for tips. When I came home my mother said, 'Right, that goes straight into the post office', and that started your savings off.

Ron Mottram

The Bread Van

Strange's bread van was a familiar sight in Latchford Village. They used to say, 'It's Strange where the bread comes from!'

Phyllis Pickering

The Errand Lad's Tale

When I left school I wanted to go and be a joiner at Warburton's, the local works. To go and learn a trade you had to serve an apprenticeship, which was from fourteen years to twenty-one years, and also you had to pay a premium. We couldn't afford to do this so that job was not to be. Then there was also an apprenticeship at Mr Mann's, the local hairdresser's. My wages would only be one shilling and sixpence so that was another job that I had to pass over. My grandma used to do some washing and cooking for Mr Henry Milling who had a big grocer's and provisions shop in Warrington and also three branch shops. She asked him if he could find me a job. I had to go and have an interview but the result was that I could start work in the warehouse as an errand boy and also help to get the orders ready to be delivered by van. I left school on the Friday and started work on Monday October 1st in 1931.

The hours were from 8.00 a.m. to 6.00 p.m. except Thursday, which was 8.00 a.m. to 1.00 p.m. and Friday, which was 8.00 a.m.

to 8.00 p.m. On my first morning I had to report to Mr Gilks who was the foreman. The warehouse was the place where ladies put the orders together and these were then checked and put into baskets ready for delivery by the vans. Each lady had to run up three flights of stairs and one down into the cellar. For the first month I was to do a lot of running up and down the stairs for the ladies who were very nice and helped me to understand what working was all about. While I was in the warehouse I got to know everything and where the different goods were kept. Sometimes the foreman would send me on a cycle to deliver a small order. This was the start of my getting used to taking the groceries to the customers.

Although there were five assistants at Milling's Latchford shop I was the youngest. There was the odd occasion when a customer would ring up and want a small order urgently. Being the youngest and able to ride a carrier cycle, I would take these

William Bridge and his trusty horse deliver Strange's bread at Bewsey just before the First World War.

Stan Smith, Milling's errand lad, poses for the camera.

the worse for drink. She was dripping wet and wearing a thin see-through underslip which was clinging to her wet skin. She just took the bottle and said, 'Wait while I get the money.' She turned round and walked through to another room and came back with her handbag. That was the last time I went there. I told the boss and he sent someone else. It took me a few days to get over that for believe me what I saw was not very nice!

I did have a few houses which I went to where the people were nice. One lady was a professional photographer and one day she asked me if I would stand with my cycle for her to take a picture. She was going to enter this in a national competition as an everyday event. I went to her house when it was dark and put on a clean coat and apron and posed with a book called *Camera* as they were the organizers of the competition. A few weeks later the lady told me that this picture was the national winner.

Stan Smith

orders out. They were mostly late in the afternoon to the big houses. Normally the van would deliver in the morning and again after dinner.

I had a few funny and not so funny experiences. One lady always rang at about five minutes to six about three times a week for a bottle of Stone's ginger wine which cost two shillings and nine pence. Since we closed at six o'clock I used to take it on my way home. The lady didn't have a maid and always paid for the bottle so that it didn't go on her weekly bill.

One night I knocked on the door and waited, then I knocked again and a voice from upstairs shouted down for me to wait a while. After a while the door opened and there stood the lady who was very big, in every sense of the word, and I'm sure she was

The Latchford Milk Cart

We used to ride in the milk cart from that farm just over the bridge. We went out with a jug for the milk and they had a ladle with a long handle. He came round every day and he always had a gang of kids on the back.

Phyllis Pickering

The Donkey Cart

In the early 1950s there was a man at Grappenhall who used to come round with a donkey cart with a milk churn. You used to take your milk out and he just used to pour it out in the street. He didn't do it for long because they altered the main road and the donkey got hurt by all the trucks going down to London and the trap got damaged as well.

Joyce Highfield

The Watercress Seller

Every morning there used to be a chap come along with a barrow selling watercress near Fennel Street where I was born.

Evelyn Barker

Shrimps for Sale

A lady came round at Latchford selling shrimps. She always had a beautiful white apron on.

Phyllis Pickering

The Potato Market

Next to the fire station at Heathside was an open space surfaced with stone sets, officially known as the Potato Market. It was better known as the Fairground because a travelling fair would spend a week there twice a year, at Christmas and Walking Day.

Each Saturday morning farmers from all over the country districts around Warrington would bring their produce to the Potato Market. The area would be covered by farm carts and lorries. Wholesalers, shop owners and market stallholders would come to buy fruit and vegetables. Usually the trading was

over by lunchtime and the farmers retired to one of the many nearby pubs. Later they set off home leaving the area littered with cabbage leaves, squashed potatoes, carrots and turnips.

An advantage of living close to the market was that late on Saturday night people could go along to the fruit and vegetable section, which would be open sometimes as late as ten o'clock, and find bargains for the weekend meal.

David Plinston

Shopping in Town

I used to go up to the Old Market on a Saturday night. There was no freezers and so everything would go off, so they'd sell the food off cheap. The fruit stalls would all be auctioning off oranges, so many pears, so much the lot. Then we'd go further down to Smart's the toffee stall and you'd get a great big bag of humbugs and boiled sweets, a tanner the lot. Then we'd go in the Meat Market and you'd get a leg of lamb for about two bob.

Milling's used to be *the* shop at Market Gate. If you went in for two pounds of sugar and a quarter of tea it would all be wrapped up in a paper with string. The service was fantastic, if you went in with a shawl on you'd get the same treatment.

Mrs Bradley

Behind the Counter in Millings

After about six months working in the warehouse of Millings I wanted a change so I asked if I could go into the shop to learn

how to serve on the counter. I was given the chance and had to wear a white coat and white apron. I went on the counter to learn how to serve bacon, ham, cheese and eggs plus other groceries. I really enjoyed this and was soon cutting bacon and had a space on the counter. From then on I used to have my regular customers who came to me.

When I was about seventeen and a half years old my boss at Milling's Warrington shop asked me to go to the branch shop in Latchford. The manager there had taken ill and the assistant manager had to take charge. This meant that they needed another assistant to take over on the bacon, cheese and ham counter. This was a promotion for me and I felt that I was

making something of my life.

Near my nineteenth birthday Mr Milling called at the Latchford shop on his weekly visit. He would always have a talk with every assistant and asked me how I would like a move to the Stockton Heath shop. I couldn't say no as this meant I would be back in my village. On the Monday morning I reported to the manager who was not very well liked by his staff. He told me what my duties were and said that I was to address him as 'Sir' at all times and also that I would not be allowed to serve on the bacon and ham counter. This was not what I was used to as the other managers had always given me the freedom to serve everyone with whatever they wanted. I am afraid I got off on the wrong foot with him. I said straight out that I would serve everything that the customer asked for as I had done at all the other branches and also at the head shop. Also I said that as we were all employed by Mr Milling we were all equal and my name was 'Stan Smith' not 'Smith'.

As it was Monday morning Mr Milling always called at the shop on the way to town and the manager saw his car arrive and went to the door and had a long talk to him. Mr Milling took us both upstairs and asked what the trouble was about and I explained. The outcome of the meeting was that the manager had to back down and the other assistants were very glad about this as they got more freedom.

I must have made a big impact on the

Time for bargains in Warrington Old Market?

manger as he got me to try my hand at window dressing. This was his pride and joy and so I felt highly honoured. The window was changed every fortnight. He asked me what about entering a competition for a window display of Kia Ora orange and lemon drinks. I said, 'Why not, we've got nothing to lose.' We both did the display and someone came and took a picture of it. After about six weeks we got a reply from this firm to the effect that we had taken first prize for the area of Lancashire and Cheshire.

Things were going along very nicely but there was something inside me saying that there was something more to be done with my life. I never had enough money in my pocket to do what the other lads of my age did. My wages at Millings were thirty shillings a week which was the average wage for all shop workers. I used to give almost all my wages to my mother to help with the upkeep at home. I smoked and had now started going to the cinema once a week. This left me with nothing at the weekend. At this time I couldn't afford to have a girlfriend. Some of my friends had motorcars and motorcycles and these were something I would have loved to have. I would always help my friends when they did any repairs and deep down I think this was what I had always wanted to do. I was always happy when I was doing something practical and I was sure I wasn't cut out to be working in a shop.

Stan Smith

The Corner Shop

Next door to Heathside School stood Mrs Green's corner shop which sold groceries, household goods of all kinds and confectionery. There were many similar shops in those days before the coming of supermarkets and hypermarkets and shopping precincts.

One piece of confectionery that went down very well (literally!) was the fairy cake. That was the name on the tray in Mrs Greens' shop but we knew them better as 'Wet Nellies'. These cakes were made from the scraps and off cuts from more expensive items in the bakery. All these bits and pieces were pressed together and made up into cakes measuring about three inches square by two inches thick and sold for half a penny. I'm sure that a boy could have survived for days on a 'Wet Nellie' for there was all the sugar and carbohydrates for energy and the sheer bulk filled the

Henry Milling, owner of a local grocery chain.

Milling's grocers and apprentices pose outside the Horsemarket Street branch in the 1900s.

stomach.

A cruel joke used to be told of a boy who was out for a walk in the country and decided to share his 'Wet Nellie' with some ducks swimming on a pond. Sometime later he knocked on the farmhouse door and told the farmer's wife, 'Missus, your ducks have sunk!'

David Plinston

Orford Lane

Orford Lane was a busy shopping area with lots of little houses. On Pinners Brow there were little tiny cottages and a little pub called the Soldiers Return on the corner. They used to have a big Maypole Dairy, fishmongers and vegetable shops. There was a cooked meat shop in Orford Lane run by a German who'd got nationalized in the First World War. He sold all kinds of roast pork, roast ham, pickled herrings and things.

Mrs Bradley

Sankey Street Co-op

The Co-op shops had what they called the centralized cash system. You made your cheque out and the customer paid you and you put it in one of those cups, turned it, pulled the handle and it used to whiz across to the cash desk. The girl took the cash out and sent the change back. At the Sankey Street store they had a system called the Lampson tube that went all round the shop.

As a boy I got in some bother with that, like lads do, playing tricks on the girls. One day I put a mouse in one of those things,

Left: *The Soldier's Return Inn on the corner of Pinner's Brow and Orford Lane.* Right: *The Old Admiral Lord Rodney Inn on the corner of Winwick Road and Pinner's Brow, around 1930.*

turned it round and sent it up to the cash desk. Of course the girl opened it and screamed in horror! The mouse was dead of course. One of my jobs as a lad was setting traps to catch the mice. That day I must have felt a bit naughty and put one in there. Instead of her getting the money as she wanted, she got a mouse. She dropped the mouse out and reported me to the boss. The next thing I heard was, 'Mr Taylor wants to see you Ron.' He said 'What's all this, Ron, have you been playing tricks on the girls?' I said, 'I'm very sorry Mr Taylor, I just couldn't help myself', and he said, 'Don't do it again!' He took it in good part. The strange thing was that the girl in the cash desk was called Lillian Innocent!

Instead of making cheques out they had what they called a climax cheque system with carbon copies. Those were the days when the Co-op paid a dividend and before Mrs Jones could get her dividend all these cheques had to be sorted. I can remember that in our cheque office there would be at least forty girls sat behind desks sorting these cheques out in order to calculate the dividend for each particular member.

I carried on in Sankey Street and in the Drapery Department until I was about twenty-one and then I applied for a First Hands job at Prestwich Co-op, which was the other side of Manchester. I left Warrington and there I got this under-manager's job. While I was there the manager became ill and I carried the shop on. Then they promoted me to manager and buyer there.

Ron Mottram

Burgess' Paper Shop

It was a little wooden hut on the corner of Forrest Street and Knutsford Road. When I was a little girl my mother sent me for a paper and I was there for ages because they couldn't see me over the counter! She'd sent me for *Family Journal* and *Titbits*.

Phyllis Pickering

Sweets

In those days sweets were nearly all displayed in cardboard boxes and you never see now the mouth-watering sweets that we had as children. There were Fairy Whispers, which were flat, different coloured shapes with writing on such as 'I love you' and 'Kiss me quick'. We had liquorice sticks, tiger nuts, Peas, Chops and Potatoes, Banana Splits, Hundreds and Thousands and Cherry Lips. It was amazing what a ha'penny in old money would buy! If we had a whole penny we were rich. We could even get into the 'Pivvie' or the Pavillion Cinema House and see a really good film for a clean empty jam jar.

Ernie Day

When Stale Cakes were a Treat

Most people remember Carter's great big café near Market Gate. Well they had another little café and shop, next to Chester's at the bottom end of Bridge Street, near Bridge Foot. I was born near there in Old Road, Latchford. When I was only a little lad and we couldn't afford to buy biscuits and stuff like that, my mother said, 'Here's a tanner [two and a half pence], go to the shop and see if you can get some stale cakes, proper cakes.' We used to go to Carter's in Bridge Street, the café, and ask if they had any stale cakes and they used to fill your basket up for a tanner with cakes that had been made the day before, or possibly the day before that.

Bill Ireland

An advertisement for the Warrington Co-operative Society.

Burgess' newsagent, tobacconist and stationers, and Singleton's butchers in Latchford village in the early 1920s.

Smart's toffee stall in Warrington Old Market.

Carter's smaller café near Bridge Foot, where Bill Ireland bought up stale cakes.

Carter's Café

I remember when my children were very tiny and I took them to Carter's Café for one cake and a glass of something. That was a treat on a Saturday morning. I'd say, 'I'll take you to Carter's Café', and they thought that was marvellous! The Winmarleigh Café in Sankey Street was even dearer still.

Vera, Laira Street Memories Group

The Winmarleigh Café

I was in service for Smith and Walker who owned the Winmarleigh Café. I used to work six days a week and sometimes on Sundays and I only got six shillings a week. The Winmarleigh Café was in Sankey Street, near Leigh Street. It was a gorgeous

shop, it was *the* café, the main one. The owners lived on Wilderspool Causeway and if you lived on Wilderspool Causeway in them days you was somebody!

Mrs Bradley

A Pantry Girl in the 1920s

I worked at the Winmarleigh Café in Sankey Street for about two years until my mother died and I was brought home. I can picture it now! Sankey Street was so narrow that you could throw from the Winmarleigh Café to Dawson's, the shop opposite.

They used to say that all the big people like businessmen went there. They had meals and early coffee there. I was training to be a pantry girl. You used to have to

65

An advertisement for Carter's.

wear a black dress and white apron. If the waitresses wanted anything they'd come and tell us.

Elsie Knight

A Mutuality Man

I came back to Warrington Co-op when I was about twenty-six. Prestwich was a smaller society than Warrington so I couldn't come back as manager in Warrington because all those jobs were filled but there was this job as mutuality collector. That was a credit system. Before I could get this job as a collector I had to supply six character references who weren't relatives. If I'd have been in any trouble I couldn't have had the job because the insurance company wouldn't have covered me. We were all insured for £1,000 in case anybody decided to take the money.

You went out of the office selling credit and collecting the money in. The credit was only for the Co-op. It was a twenty week club. We issued them with vouchers which they could go and spend in the shop. If the voucher was for £5 they'd pay it back at one shilling a week. As inflation went on that shilling became two shillings, three shillings and then five shillings and so it went on. You gave them the credit to buy things but the secret was knowing your people. You were only allowed one per cent bad debts. If you got more than one per cent they took you off the job.

In those days you could knock on the door and if there was no answer you could open it. You'd go in lots of houses and your money and card were on the sideboard waiting for you. You'd go into some houses and there'd be gold watches, rings as well as money on the sideboard but obviously you didn't touch them. People didn't bother about you going in and just taking the money without anybody being there. Imagine doing that these days! It was trust you see between one and another.

Ron Mottram

Workers at Richmond's Shandos in the 1920s.

The Scullery Maid

I was fifteen when I went to work in the kitchens at Walton Hall – that would be about 1935. I mostly did the vegetables for the servants' hall and the dining room. I had to cook all the servants' hall breakfast and the housekeeper's room breakfast. Then we used to help Miss Musson the cook making all the sauces and other kinds of things we had to do when all the family was at home. We were doing practically the same kinds of things as Miss Musson. You had to get all the things ready for the oven, like grouse and all the game birds. I had to pluck all those as a scullery maid. They used to leave wild ducks until they were high. I've seen the ducks moving from side to side because they were full of maggots – and they would eat them like that!

Another larder had great black stone slabs in it where they used to put things like fish to keep cold. Then there was the dairy where Mr Rowe used to churn butter on Thursdays. They had cows down at the shippons near the bridge, where they put the toilets later. The cows kept us in milk and butter and cream. Every Thursday morning before breakfast we had to clean all the copper things on the kitchen shelves. There were all sorts of things like jelly moulds and great big preserving pans.

A break from housework for the Walton Hall servants in the early 1930s. May Green is standing on the far right.

Lady Daresbury would have a big dinner party when it was the Grand National, perhaps twenty guests or something like that. We had to be on our toes then! Miss Musson used to get her hair off! She used to get all worked up and then we'd have to watch out or else we'd cop it for what she did wrong. We didn't do as much in advance as they do now. They had a small fridge but I don't think they had any freezers. Miss Musson did quite a few dishes that came with all sorts of sauces and things on that we didn't have at home in those days.

Miss Musson did have a cookery book but Lady Daresbury would come to the kitchen at ten o'clock to see the menu and tell them what she wanted. They used to have a lot of pheasants and duck and once a year, when it was hunting season, somebody would send venison from Scotland. I remember we used to cook it in a great big pastry, like dough that you made for bread. We'd bake it in the oven in a tin and the pastry would keep all the juices in. It was lovely and tender when it was done. Miss Musson would make all sorts of things with minced pheasant and a lot of it was used in the servants' hall. If they had a pheasant they'd only just take the breast off. They wouldn't touch the legs or anything like that. There was never any shortage of anything. If something spoilt, there was always something else to send in.

May Green

The Estate Joiner

We did all kinds of work up at Walton Hall. We hung doors and windows and we made stairs, doors and panel doors. We bought nothing, it was all hand worked, no machines. We did the type of joinery that most joiners wouldn't contemplate today, like country joinery work. With shippon work you had to know the sizes relevant to cattle, like the bings that were put in between the head of the cattle and the passageway where they put the straw. You had to know all these sizes, fittings and that. Short beds, longer ones, heel trees, deeper one to keep the cattle clean. Then we did barrow work, wheelwrighting, making wheels and things like that. You made your own pole ladders, special ladders where the spindles or rungs were turned by hand.

A door was considered a good day's work. You'd start off with it rough sawn, nothing touched and you'd face that door up. You'd start at six in the morning and finish at five at night. You'd plane the stuff off, mortice it and tenon it. It was all by hand, all hand tools. All we had was what we called 'britches arse power', nothing else!

Fred Kippax

Laundry Maids

There were only two working in the laundry at Walton Hall in the 1930s. They did nothing else, only that every day. On Thursday they had a woman come in to do all the sheets off the servants' beds. She lived up at Moore and her husband worked on the estate. They still used the old box mangle, a big old wooden thing. Mr Rowe, the odd job man, used to help them by doing a lot of mangling for them. They had a sort

Miss Musson (left), the Walton Hall cook, at work in her kitchen.

of washing machine. It was wooden and had a wooden lid with a handle on the top which Mr Rowe used to turn. It had the same action as a washing machine but they had to manhandle it themselves.

They had electric irons but they still used some that were heated on a stove. I can remember Hilda, the head laundry maid, using all sorts of little irons; tiny ones for doing frills and collars, and it was mostly those that she used to heat on this stove. Goffering, as they called it, for frills and pillow cases. They used the box mangle for the Servants' Hall sheets but they ironed the best ones for the family. There were about six racks: big iron things on wheels that were in heated cupboards. They used to hang all the things on the racks, push them in the cupboard and shut the door to do the airing.

May Green

A Warrington Tailoress

Mother learned her trade with Mrs Burton, a lady who ran a high-class dressmaking business at her home in Manchester Road in the row of houses opposite the cemetery and adjoining the public house on the corner of Padgate Lane.

The apprentices worked for the first years of their training without payment as being taught their trade was considered a sufficient reward. Some other places used to charge a premium for the tuition. They were only paid a full wage on the completion of their apprenticeship at twenty-one years of age, if competent. Their working hours were unlimited, starting at 8.00 a.m. and finishing in the evening when the day's task was completed. Regardless of this mother

always spoke of these as happy days, spent working there with the girls in the homely atmosphere of the Burton household. Mother's wage went to the family budget, so that she did more sewing at home at night for people so that she could have some money of her own.

At this time she lived with her family [the Rathbones] at Paddington Lock. She left Mrs Burton's on marriage, when she and dad came to live in Sankey's Cottages on Padgate Lane and mother started her own business there. Then I came on the scene in 1906.

The dresses she made were chosen from designs and patterns from the fashion magazines. *Weldon's Fashions* was one I remember. The materials were usually bought from retail shops in Warrington, such names as Dutton, Grimes, Craik and Williams come to mind – Mr Grimes' shop was on the corner of Academy and Buttermarket Streets. She used silk, satin, taffeta, crêpe de Chine and others, with the appropriate linings to match. Also canvas, wadding, net and buckram, which was a very stiff canvas used to make the waistbands.

Then there were the trimmings of various types and braid, beads, sequins, cottons and silks; press studs, hooks and eyes and wooden centres for hand-made buttons and strips of whalebone of various lengths for collars and the waist.

I can remember the tools she used: an Imperial treadle-driven sewing machine – how it used to whirr! – and a dummy, adjustable for modelling the garments on. Then there were the goffering and crimping irons which were heated and used for fancy pleating, usually on the bodice fronts, and also the needles, pins, bodkins, buttonhole and larger scissors, a stiletto for making holes, several thimbles and various sizes of heavy pressing irons.

Mother had plenty of orders to work on and with the assistance of her younger sister – another product of the Burton stable –made coats, costumes, wedding dresses and fancy dresses with leg-of-mutton sleeves and high necks and ankle length skirts, usually to be seen at the frequent dances held in Padgate School.

Then there were the mourning orders at short notice, usually rush jobs, sometimes entailing work going on until the early hours to get the garments ready in time to wear for the funeral. It was a must for all the family to wear black, paid for out of the insurance money. These dresses were usually adorned with plenty of black crêpe. The insurance was paid at an old penny a week for life with about £10.00 received on the death of the insured.

Mother's charges for the making of dresses ranged from 3s 6d to 5s plus the cost of the material.

John Davies

Mrs Davies the tailoress.

Hand Velvet Cutting

I worked at the United Velvet Cutters in Hale Street. I started work in 1928 at the age of fifteen and my wages were six shillings and four pence. I worked from quarter to eight in the morning until five thirty at night. I had a five minute break at eleven o'clock in the morning and I had to 'scramble' for lunch. I also worked until lunchtime on Saturdays.

Our supervisor was Alice Lomax and the foreman was called Fred Rothwell. If we had to call him because we had a problem he would say, 'I can't come for an hour yet, I mean an hour and a half', and we were on piece work.

We cut the fustian by hand using a knife with a guide on the end. The fustian cloth came in bales from Manchester. It was stretched on machines about twelve to fourteen feet long, over slow moving conveyor belts. We walked up and down beside it, cutting the pile to make cotton velvet.

Our boss, Mr Carmichael, was a very humane man to work for. He would come in at half past eight to see if all his workers were happy. If we weren't singing he'd ask who'd upset us. Some of the workers carried on until they were in their seventies.

We were paid Wednesday to Wednesday and it was a well-paid job. You could earn a basic seven to ten shillings a week, perhaps

71

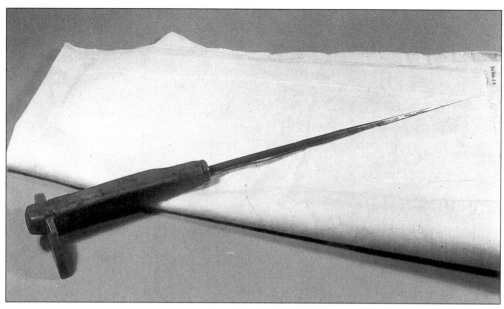

A fustian cutter's knife used to cut open the loops on the surface of the velvet-like cloth.

even a pound and we were paid extra for each piece we cut. Each piece was 365 yards long – 'days in a year' they used to call it. It took us three days to cut a piece but you got your pay docked if you made any errors, or slips as they were called.

If you made a bad slip you'd cover it up by getting the material caught in the machine. Then we'd tell the mechanics to keep away to stop them finding out. When we'd finished the piece it would be taken to the mending room to have the holes repaired.

During the war I left to work in munitions and then I got the best job I ever had, working at SDP, or Speed and Prompt Delivery. They were a Liverpool firm based at the back of the old Marks and Spencer's shop off Mill Street. We had to salvage soap and margarine cartons which were then sorted into batches of about fifty.

Margaret Delaney

Mechanized Velvet Cutting

I was no stranger to the world of the velvet cutting shop. It was situated in Hale Street and I lived nearby. It was a fascinating place and every afternoon after school we would go and watch the women in the workroom. I thought it was a wonderful job where you could walk between the frames in your bare feet!

In those days the velvet was cut by hand using a knife and guide. The only light came from a candle placed at each end of the frame. Before the material reached the cutters it went to the stiffening shop. Here the material was treated with a paste-like solution and I've known people to use this solution when they were decorating. My mother worked for a time in the stiffening shop.

After it had been treated the material put on rolls. These were taken to the cutting shop and fed onto the frames while they were hung from the ceiling. The women worked long hours in the cutting shop and I have seen babies brought in to be fed and then taken home again.

At the age of thirteen I had to leave school as others did in those days because of family circumstances. I had to obtain a copy of my birth certificate and on the back was printed the reason for needing the certificate: 'work'.

By this time a new velvet cutting shop had been opened by a Mr Netherwood from Yorkshire. It was situated further down Hale Street, nearer the bridge. The method used there of cutting velvet was something of a revolution because, although a knife and guide were still used, the whole process was run by electricity. We started work at eight o'clock in the morning and worked until half past five. If, however, we were very busy then we started at half past six.

I started on one frame while I was learning. My wage was ten shillings a week. Once you had learned how to do the job you got the basic ten shillings a week plus piece money. This did not mean that you always took home a substantial wage by any means. If you happened to get a bad piece of material on your frame it could take a week, or maybe more, to do the work. During that time you only got your basic ten shillings. Many a night I've gone home in tears because I couldn't get my piece right!

Women had the job of mending the holes in the velvet. They were always known as 'enders and menders'. We looked forward to getting the velvet to cut for Lewis' Store. This was always a pleasure to work on and you knew that you were in for a good week when you had what was called AL velvet. When I got married in 1929 I was out of work. I did, however, buy the velvet for my wedding dress at Lewis' for just over twelve shillings a yard.

I was asked to go back to the cutting shop during the war. At this time only half the building was being used by Salford Electric and I was only working part-time. The method of cutting had not changed but now we were working on four frames at a time.

Mary McHugh

Going to Work

They used to cut through Hale Street from Winwick Road to Orford Lane to get to the factory at Cockhedge Mills. You could hear them going past each morning with their clogs on. There was an old lady, Mrs Cotterill, who used to come in the morning and knock you up. I think you used to pay her three pence a week. She came round with a long pole like a cane and tap on the upstairs window. I don't think we had any alarm clocks in those days so it was a regular thing. You knew very well if you didn't get up then you'd miss your work.

Mrs Bradley

The Knocker-Up

Where I lived in James Street, at the top was the factory and I could hear the factory workers go by with their clogs on. The lamplighter used to come and the knocker-up. My dad worked on the railways and the railway knocker-up would come any hour of the day. The door was never locked and he used to walk in and say, 'Mr Sharp, on at once for Carlisle!' He'd come to the bottom of the stairs and shout my dad.

My mother-in-law used to knock-up

round Earl Street and Cyril Street. She had a prop with wire on the top and she used to knock on the window. She used to get two pence a week for getting up at four in the morning and this was between the wars.

Ada Bate

A Cotton Weaver's Tale

I started work at Armitage and Rigby's Cockhedge Mill when I was thirteen years old. As a helper to a four-loom weaver I had to carry the finished cloth to the warehouse and bring the weft from the warehouse whenever it was needed. My wages were three shillings and sixpence a week. That was paid to me by the four-loom weaver who I worked for. If she had no change I had to wait for it until Saturday. After two years I was put on two looms and my wages then were between one pound and one pound and ten shillings a week.

Work began at 6.00 a.m. every morning and finished at 5.30 p.m. on Mondays to Fridays and at twelve noon on Saturday. We had half an hour for breakfast and one hour for dinner. We had no entertainment in the evening and had to be in bed by nine o'clock each night and up at five o'clock in the morning.

The factory gates were closed at six o'clock and everybody who was late had their names taken and lost a quarter hour's pay – 'quartered' as we called it. There were no tea breaks and if you were seen talking you were sent home.

We cleaned the looms during meal times so we could keep the looms running. There was no rest room and if anybody was hurt they went to the joiner's shop where they received first aid, if the joiner was in.

We carried the finished 'cuts' of cloth on our shoulder to the warehouse where they were weighed and examined. If there were any spots of oil we had to go to the warehouse to clean them off. Any faults and we were fined various amounts between two pence and a shilling. If there was any breakdown of the mill engine all looms stopped – and so did our pay.

After the First World War we had the slump and went on three days a week. The other three days we signed on at the Labour Exchange. Every day at the Labour Exchange there would be a long queue. A lot of people were out of work and everybody who was working was on short time. We were often in the queue for up to two hours.

Friday evenings we finished work at 5.30 p.m. We had to run to the Exchange to draw out of work pay. More often than not it would be seven o'clock when I arrived home for tea.

Mrs E. Hatton

Working at Cockhedge

I started work at Cockhedge in 1915 at the age of thirteen. My first wages were three shillings and then a lot of the men went to the war and that was my chance to get on a machine. My first big wages were six shillings and that was a lot of money then. One or two of the other workers were what we called 'flomping'. That meant helping yourself to your own money. When it was the breakfast half hour they'd say, 'How much are you flomping? I'm going to take so much out for my pocket money because I want to go to the pictures.' I had an older sister there and she knew what we got so

A view of Cockhedge Spinning Mill from the roof of the weaving department.

all my money had to be handed to mother.

After I'd been there for a long while they picked me to give tours to visitors so I had to learn what was going on in each section. The raw cotton came as bales to the cotton shed and these were broken open by a man with an axe. Then the big pieces of cotton were taken away in a wheelbarrow or a skip to the carding room which was on the bottom floor. Next you went up to the ring rooms where the mules spun long bobbins of cotton and later the smaller bobbins which went on the shuttles in the weaving shed. As it went from machine to machine the thread got narrower. The spinners were all on piece work so if they had a broken end they'd take the bobbin out, take the thread and twist it and make it one piece again, without stopping the machine.

Next you went to the weaving shed and that was all on one floor. When I first went there you learned on two looms and if you were quick on your job you went to four looms. A long time later they worked on six looms and I believe that before I finished they was on twenty-four looms. I said to our boss, 'One woman can't see to twenty four looms, coming up and down and seeing what's going on!' At one time the weaver had to have a helper to sweep her loom and when the bobbins were finished she had to go to a little warehouse and pick up a box of new ones. The helper was doing all the dirty work but say an end [of cotton] broke the weaver was supposed to train the girl how to piece up.

After the weaver had finished a piece of cloth it went to the picking room where they looked it over to pick out the flaws and then it went on a big machine to be folded. From there it went to the warehouse for the buyers to see and then it went to other mills. If there were any pieces with flaws in that was cut off and the workers could buy it.

Ethel Whitfield

Inside the weaving sheds at Cockhedge Mill, where for once the looms are silent.

Making Sole Leather

I was Works Manager at the Central Tanneries at Howley from 1934 until the tannery closed in 1960. Producing leather for shoe soles began by soaking and liming the dry hides. Dry hides were imported into this country from many parts of the world and hides from cattle slaughtered here were also used. The greatest risk in handling imported hides was contracting anthrax and great care was taken to have any doubtful pimple or boil fully investigated. We would even go to Fazakerley Hospital in Liverpool where expert opinion and treatment was available.

The dry hides had to be got back to their natural condition and this was done by soaking them in water for seven days, then drawing them out of the pit and piling them flat overnight. Between sixty and eighty hides were then transferred to a pit from which a pack of hides had been drawn. This was called 'an old lime'. The hides were then drawn up one by one the next day and drawn down again. All the drawing was done with a sharp pointed hook on the end of a six-foot ash sapling. This first lifting of the hides in the old lime was called 'the first draw'.

On the second draw the old lime liquor was drained off – into the drain connected to the River Mersey no less! A new lime liquor was made which consisted of one hundred weight of lime which was thoroughly slaked in a tub or lime box. This was then run into the pit with about 800 gallons of water, making sure that no unslaked pieces went into the pit as these would have burnt the hides. A two-gallon bucket was then filled with sodium sulphide crystals and these were liquefied by blowing live steam into the bucket. The sodium sulphide solution was then added to the pit, all plunged up and the pack of hides were drawn in one by one. The third or finish draw was made after two days and after another two days the seven-day liming process was completed and the hides were ready for unhairing.

Loosening the hair was partly achieved by the action of the lime and partly by the action of the sodium sulphide which speeded up the process. Sodium sulphide was the cause of the awful smell in the lime yard of the tanneries, until you got used to it of course. The blood and dung on the hides also played a part.

The decision after liming was whether the hair was fit for sale and with English hides this was always the case. The hides were therefore put through an unhairing machine. Here the hides were thrown onto a rubber bolster and clamped whilst a revolving blunt-bladed cylinder moved down and up it. The hide was then turned around and the other half unhaired. The hair was collected at the bottom.

The dry hides were put into a revolving drum with water and perhaps half a bucket of dissolved sodium sulphide to ensure they were completely unhaired. After twenty minutes the door was changed to a perforated one and with the action of running water the hides were then cleaned and ready for transfer to the fleshing machine.

The blade of the fleshing machine was a ten-foot long steel-bladed cylinder

Dry hides arriving at Howley Tannery.

travelling at about 1,500 revs per minute. A pneumatic cylinder took care of the unequal thickness of the hide when the fleshy side of the hide was pressed against the blade. This resulted in a nice clean hide which was then given a further wash in clean water. It was then ready for rounding, which meant cutting it into a butt, a shoulder and two bellies. All were then ready for deliming and tanning.

Jack Hamlett

Women in the Tanneries

I worked in Fleming's Tannery just the other side of Battersby Lane. They made heavy leather for soles. I worked on the tanning pits and I wore leggings of a rough wrap tied with string and a leather apron.

Men pulled the soaking wet hides out of the pits and I put the wringing wet hides through a big squeezer to get all the tannin out. Then I went on polishing. You used to put the massive bends, or sides, through this steel and it polished them. Then they were hung upstairs and it was boiling hot. We used to hang whole sides of leather on hooks in a big long shed. A man used to wax them. It was very, very heavy work and terribly dirty but there were mostly women working in the tannery.

The tan pits were massive deep square or oblong yards which were covered over. The men used to drag the hides out with hooks. I've seen men fall in many a time. I don't know how I managed to do the work. You used to put the hides on a bogey that was taller than me and then push with all your might. I don't think I was paid above three pounds a week.

Women workers at Waring's tannery on the hide cutting machines, 1930s.

The packing room at Crosfields, which was regarded as a good firm to work for.

I had no husband in work so I had to work to bring up my four children. It didn't matter what kind of work it was, I'd just tackle it. There was no such thing as Social Security or Family Allowance then. My husband worked on the railways and he'd had an accident but there was no compensation. He was in hospital and you only got about ten shillings a week in sick pay. Nearly all the women had to work. There was a time in the big Depression in the 1930s when you'd tackle any job you could.

Mrs Bradley

Working at Crosfields

I worked at Crosfields from the age of sixteen. My dad, auntie and uncles helped me to get a job there. You had to know somebody who'd push for you. I worked in the vegetable oil section and we'd cross over the river with the men in a barge, going over in a morning and coming back at night.

When we worked this side of the river we went in the print department making Persil boxes. They were ready cut and stacked and we had to slide them along and make up the boxes to be filled with the Persil powder.

I swam for Crosfields and I was in the St John's Ambulance Brigade but I was never in the opera. I worked there until I got married at the age of twenty and had to leave. We got a case full of the cream of their products. I've still got the case but it's a bit battered now!

Elsie Baird

The Monks, Hall & Co. steelworks, seen from the River Mersey.

A Child's View of Monks Hall

Grandma Thomas, my Mam's mother, came from Brierley Hills as a young lady and met and married John Thomas, a shoemaker's son from North Wales. They raised a family of eight children and lived in Wellfield Street, only a few minutes walk from our house in Lancaster Street. Grandad Thomas worked at Monks Hall Steelworks and one of my most pleasant memories is of me taking his supper to Monk's, as it was known.

Grandma would get it ready, put it in a basin with an enamel plate on top and wrap the whole thing in a big red and white spotted handkerchief for me to carry, along with a bottle of cold tea. I remember too that she used to put me five or six new potatoes in a piece of paper with a bit of butter on top for me to eat as I went along.

When I got to Monk's steelworks I always knew where to find my grandad. I will never forget that magical place – or so it seemed to me at the time – where huge, hot slabs of metal were rolled into sheets. At night in the dimly lit mills the sparks would shoot off like fireworks from the glow of the metal. It was very hard work and grandad was literally wet through with sweat, and this was all through his working life.

Ernie Day

Richmonds in the 1930s

When I started work at Richmonds in the '30s the Harris family used to pick up pig iron from Latchford Railway Station and take it to Richmonds by horse and cart. Then it was placed on the pig bank there for moulding and casting.

There was the core shop where they made the cores for things like the gas burners. The mill room was where there were barrels and you used to mix the enamel. Another part was the shot-blasting department where they used to clean all the castings. The shot was very fine pellets fired under great pressure through a fine nozzle to clean big components. The men went in a diver's suit and air was pumped into them. I worked on the air vents which used to extract the fumes. You also had the spray department and the mottling department, where they used sponges for mottling. That was all part of the Chandos.

Only one department was on shift work and that was the enamelling department. When I started working at Richmonds I clocked on at half past five and if you were late you were quartered. With overtime you could get nine or ten hours in. The enamelling department was the worst paid for a man. The top rate then in the 1930s

was about £2 16s 0d for an apprentice sheet metal worker.

But Richmonds was ahead of its time because there was piece work there in the '30s before anybody ever spoke of it. It was time and motion you know and you had to cut out the motion as much as possible. You wouldn't have to pick up your metal; your labourer would do that for you.

I went to work on a bike and then all of a sudden they did away with the trams and took buses up there. It was a great occasion for people coming from across town who could now get a bus right through to work, right to the top just by the hydraulic shed.

In the '30s you could swim in Latchford Locks, above the locks. In the summertime when we were working overtime or at dinner time we'd go and have a swim. The Ship Canal was handy

Richmond's moulding shop in the early 1920s.

A Richmond's outing on the Manchester Ship Canal with the works in the background.

for Richmonds because it carried the goods.

Before the war Richmonds and Fletcher Russell were separate and they were at daggers drawn. Then they formed the Radiation Group which included Glovers and quite a number of other firms and the headquarters were in London. Fletchers were on their own for many years. They had their own cricket team and Richmonds had their own cricket team. Fletcher Russell used to play their cricket on Chester Road where Alan Cobham and many others used to come with The Flying Circus. That was also Whitecross Rec. as well and that was where St James' church used to have their entertainment on Walking Day.

Walter Norris

The Status of Wire Drawers

Wire drawers used to walk around with their best serge suits on, a gold guard across their chest and a gold watch on. They had Best Rooms in the pubs. They put a penny extra on the drinks over the bar price to keep the rank and file out. A gill of beer was only two and a half pence, so to put a penny on that was a certain way of keeping you out. They had Best Rooms exclusively for wire drawers or anybody that they cared to accept into them. It was more or less a private room within a public house. Labourers would no more dream of going in a Best Room than they would of flying. This applied all over Warrington because of all the wire works. There was Rylands in Church Street; there was Whitecross Wire Drawing works on the Liverpool Road side; there was the Firth on

Howley side; there was Lockers; Greenings; and Longford Wire. The wire drawers had this status that went with the lolly.

The wire drawers looked down on you that much that when I was labouring at Rylands they wouldn't take me into their union. They had their own Wire Drawers and Kindred Workers Union. They wouldn't have organized labourers in at all then. They'd let you labour for them, they'd let you clean up for them and clean the boilers up. There was a caste system; they were the wire drawers and you were labourers and never the twain shall meet. There was no communication with them. It was like all craftsmen. If you were a fitter or a joiner, a brickie or an electrician there was very little communication between them and the working man – apart from labouring for them. There wasn't many craftsmen that I

knew that had a social conscience because they'd been brought up in that relatively privileged situation. They'd got that extra quid, which was the difference between their standard of living and yours. They lived in a better standard of housing than the labouring classes, broadly speaking, and that relatively privileged position gave them a different perspective on life.

Harry Hardman

Keeping Check of the Workers

When I started work at the Castle Rubber Works at the age of fourteen there was no clock, you used to go to the lodge window and they gave you a tally out of a little cup. When you went home you gave them back.

Inside Rylands Wire works, off Church Street, in the early 1900s.

At last, tea breaks are allowed at Rylands!

You used to go and get your pay with this little tally thing as well. If you were late you were 'quarter houred' and lost a quarter hour's pay.

Margaret Barlow

No Tea Breaks Allowed

When I worked at Rylands in Academy Street we weren't allowed a break at all. We worked from quarter to eight until half past twelve. We used to sneak into the toilets but the foreman came in and hoisted us all out. We were only teenagers.

He used to visit the general office so we'd say, 'Come on, he's gone!' We'd just brewed the tea one day and he turned back. He emptied it all away, every bit. Oh, it was cruel because it was freezing and we used to wear old coats to keep warm. What's more

he hid the teapot and the cups. Well, we looked everywhere and eventually we found them down in a big drainpipe. The thinnest one had to get right in and get everything back again. Really I think he was just frightened of losing his own job.

Phyllis Pickering

CHAPTER 7

Politics and Hard Times

Lady Greenall (centre) speaks out for the Conservatives.

Working Class Tories

You could knock on some doors and they'd be bigoted Tories. In some instances the poorer they were, the more Tory they were because they looked up to the establishment to solve their problems. They used to touch their cap to Lady Greenall, touch their forelock. She used to come round at election time dishing blankets out but she only came at election time.

On Cockhedge there were probably the worst slums in Warrington. An old socialist who brought me up was canvassing on Cockhedge in the 1920s when the Labour Party was coming. He was trying to explain the difference. He was at a pretty grim place and the front door was propped off its hinges. He shouted, 'I've come here for the Labour Party.' A voice answered, 'Who? Come in.' When he went in there was a fellow sitting there eating and drinking on this orange box

– that was his furniture. This socialist thought this was fertile ground and started preaching the gospel. When he stopped the fellow said, 'Are you one of those Whacker-outer-ers? Are you going to take everything off us and whack it out to all the others?' That was his idea of a socialist!

Harry Hardman

Lady Greenall

I remember during the election time everybody's window used to be all dressed up. There was no Labour Party then, there was only Conservatives or Liberals. My mother and father were very big Unionists [Conservatives].

I remember one day when they were electioneering and my mother went to the door in her shirt blouse and her apron made from rough wrapping. There was Lady Greenall who got out of her black and yellow trap. My mother said, 'Come in', and I'll always remember that my dad was having kippers. We had a big square table in the middle of the room and as there was no polished tables in those days my mother had put a newspaper underneath so that my dad wouldn't dirty the tablecloth. My mother said, 'Will you have a kipper?' and Lady Greenall said, 'Oh, I will!' so she sat there at the table eating this kipper. My mother told her she could wash her hands in the back kitchen if she liked because there was a towel in there and I said, 'Mam, mam!' in horror. But my mother said, 'Nay, she's no different than us.' Lady Greenall said, 'I've enjoyed that.' She was a lovely person, a lady.

Mrs Bradley

The formidable Lady Greenall attracted a grudging respect from her Labour opponents on the campaign trail.

The Blighty Club

By and large the Greenalls did a lot of things people don't realize. At Christmas time they'd get someone, a butcher, to kill a bullock. Any organization in Warrington would be told to deliver it to where it was needed. No one ever knew where it came from. The same thing with blankets and things like that.

During the First World War Lady Greenall ran the Blighty Club in Sankey Street and she was in France for the whole of three years solid, in the front line,

The Blighty Club in Sankey Street was opened by Lady Greenall in the First World War as a social centre for the local armed forces.

providing comforts for the troops like tea, coffee and smokes at her own expense.

Fred Kippax

A Land Fit for Heroes

I was in the Labour Party from being in the Labour League of Youth at the age of ten or eleven. After the 1914-18 war the fight was over between the Conservatives and Liberals, nationally and locally. After the First World War we knew something was going on, you could feel it. The Labour Party were starting to campaign as opposed to the Conservatives and Liberals. Working people had to vote for one or the other, there was nothing else. Working people could be bitterly Conservative or Liberal and be prepared to fight about it –

and they did! Then the Labour Party started to grow because during the First World War we were going to have 'a country fit for heroes to live in'. That was part of the propaganda to recruit men into the army. They were volunteers in the First World War until they brought in conscription very late on, about 1916 or '17. Millions of lads just joined up. They were going to see the Germans off in about three weeks and have fun and games with the girls in France!

The Labour Party started to be acceptable to a lot of people and the policies that they were putting forward. The trade unions had been accepted in 1914-18 by the establishment, instead of fighting them, to get the war won. Trade union membership went through the roof. Firms were giving them facilities to get the war won.

The reality was after the war was over they were trying to push everybody back to square one. Millions were unemployed again in the early 1920s. Lads stood on street corners, arms off, blinded by the war, begging. I can see them now.

The Labour movement was strong in Warrington but we still had a Tory and Liberal council. We had the first Labour MP in 1923, a chap called Dukes, Charles Dukes, who became Lord Dukeston – God forgive him, I won't! He was preaching socialism in the 1920s, that was the attraction. When you got the reality – back to unemployment, back to poverty, rickets, tuberculosis, all diseases of poverty – then the lads that knew the score would say, 'A land fit for heroes to live in? You've got to be bloody heroes to live in it!' We got a Labour government in the 1923

election and they'd never come a mile near that before.

At the age of eleven I became politically active in the Labour Party delivering literature, snatching numbers outside polling booths. I remember in the 1923 election – I'd be about fourteen – the Independent Labour Party was the propagandist wing of the Labour movement and they had a lorry from somewhere. I was on this, going round, shouting, trying to stir the voters. We'd do anything. It was a movement not an organization. Inside you it was something different and you knew it was right. It was a religion with the old socialists. There was no money in it for anybody and there was no peerages; only work and dedication, that's what appealed to me. I'd been brought up as a Christian and I went

Charles Dukes (centre), Warrington's first Labour MP, who later accepted a peerage, to the disgust of many party workers.

to Sunday school three times a day and I went to a Church of England day school. I was pretty well indoctrinated with the religious theory of Christianity. The pioneers and the propagandists preached a socialism that I could equate with Christianity and the Brotherhood of Man.

There were meetings outside 'on the stump' as they used to call it. I joined the ILP after the Young Socialists because I thought the Labour Party wasn't going fast enough. That's the natural reaction of youth! We could see them moving towards the establishment: McDonald, Snowden and the others. Moving towards the fleshpots. We joined the ILP which was affiliated to the Labour Party but was the propagandist wing. Some of the propagandists of the ILP used to make my blood run cold. You'd think they were prophets out of the Bible, preaching a gospel. The basic difference between their socialism and the Bible was, 'We want it here, while we're living.'

The ILP wasn't strong in Warrington but they were influential as they had dedicated and intelligent men. The Labour Party treated the ILP as the workhorses. We could do the donkey work at election time. I've canvassed every ward in this town. I lived in St John's Ward and that was the first ward that went Labour because it contained all these Irish people on Cockhedge. The Labour Party attracted those that had got the worst end of the stick. That was 1921-22.

Charles Dukes was returned as Labour MP at the end of 1923 [Parliament didn't reconvene until 1924] and when he went to London there was a torchlight procession from the Labour Club in Church Street to Bank Quay Station.

Harry Hardman

The Pawn Shop

Poverty was a real threat to many families and each Monday morning there used to be a continual procession of poor wretched women taking their prized possessions to the local pawnbrokers. This was Arthur Leigh, whose shop was in Baxter Street. The practice was to take their Sunday Best clothes out of pawn on a Friday or Saturday, wear them on Sunday and then take them back into pawn on a Monday.

Ernie Day

Public Assistance

I got ten shillings a week sick pay for my husband and I had good parents who helped as far as they could. I remember going down to the Board of Guardians, where the registrar's is now, in Museum Street and got a food ticket. I turned it over and it said on the back what you could have and where you could go for it. I stood outside Milling's shop in Horsemarket Street waiting for people to go out before I'd go in. I'll never forget how humiliating it was having this food ticket. Then they said, 'Come back next week and we'll put your case before the committee.' I went on the Thursday and there were hundreds there. I was in the wrong queue so I had to queue up again. They did give me the money but it was awful.

I was brought up never to waste anything and I made everything that the children wore on an old treadle sewing machine. They were always neat and clean. Them that couldn't cope had no shoes and they'd be running around in their bare feet. My dad would buy pieces of leather and mend their

Originally opened as the post office, this building on the corner of Sankey Street and Winmarleigh Street served as the Labour Exchange during the 1920s.

shoes. The police had a fund for poor children and would buy them trousers, jerseys and clogs. The poorer ones got taken in the workhouse where the hospital is over Froghall Bridge. Everybody was up against it. I've seen men fight in our backs if one had got a shift and the other thought he should have had it. They'd fight over who should have a shift at the forge.

Mrs Bradley

The Means Test

I was on the dole in the 1930s and in the ILP we used to sign on and hold a meeting outside the Labour Exchange. The people that were in work shunned us because we were out of work. We'd hold meetings right outside the Labour Exchange. There was a piece of land outside the Tory Club in Sankey Street, opposite the Town Hall.

I was means tested and I got nowt. They used to check the total income coming in the house and if it was over a very basic level father kept son, brother or daughter. Lads left home to escape it. They'd go and find lodgings somewhere and they'd get a few bob then because they wasn't living with the family. They'd lodge with an old woman in a back room. They'd get five shillings or maybe ten bob if they were lucky.

We had demonstrations to the Public Assistance Committee, parades around the town, demanding work or maintenance.

Harry Hardman

CHAPTER 8

The Second World War

The Revd Edward Downham leads the victory celebrations at St Paul's church, Bewsey, in 1945.

Gas Masks for Babies

War was declared by the time we moved to Dover Road. I remember the radio announcement on 3 September 1939. All the neighbours came out into the street to talk. I suppose they were all fearful what war would bring.

I hated the blackout. Everywhere had to be heavily curtained. The air raid wardens patrolled when the sirens sounded to make sure there was no chink of light anywhere. My eldest sister was married by that time and she gave birth to a daughter on 5 September. This daughter was Latchford's first war baby. I disliked the gas masks we had. The one for a baby was a large bag type. The baby was put inside and the mask had to be pumped by hand to supply a constant air supply. Luckily they were never needed for real.

Ette Fresle

Family Life in the Second World War

The Second World War brought tremendous changes to my life. I was five years old at the outbreak and I vaguely remember we were on holiday on the Isle of Man and had to return home. My father was called up and served in the Royal Navy. At the age of twenty-four my mother was forced into munitions work at Risley as it was considered that my grandmother who had thirteen children – three of them younger than me – could look after my brother and myself during the day! To give her her due she did her best not to differentiate between her own children and her grandchildren. I well remember her scrupulously dividing a couple of oranges between us.

My mother learned to cope with food rationing and eventually she moved from the factory floor into the offices, like many women who took it for granted that they would always work outside the home. They enjoyed it even though not all of them had the support of their husbands. My father didn't object too much as he was sensible enough to accept that two wages were tremendously helpful. However, my mother still did the bulk of the housework. She took charge of both wages, giving Father his pocket money and being totally responsible for the payment of the bills. I think the Second World War altered everything as far as the place of women in society was concerned.

Audrey Lewis

Air Raid Shelters

The air raid shelter was down under the ground at Raddon Court on Knutsford

Warrington's Air Raid Precautions Wardens (ARPs) stand ready at Orford with stirrup pump and first aid kits at hand.

Road. When we were going to Bolton Council School if the sirens went the police were there to take you in. That was the main air raid shelter and it was all brick built tunnels. We spent the morning down there singing, 'Nick Nack, Paddy Whack, give a dog a bone...'

Joan Blears

The Brewery Warning System

They had baskets on the turrets of the old Greenalls' Brewery, on Wilderspool Causeway, to say what kind of air raid it was. One was for gas and then they had a green one that they put up when the air raid was finished.

Wendy Wiles

A Bridge Too Far

We went to Stockton Heath School from Loushers Lane and as soon as the sirens went they stopped the swing bridge so that it lay along the Manchester Ship Canal. This was so that it couldn't be seen and get bombed. If we were stuck that side we were stuck inside school and couldn't get home.

Mavis Holt

Man the Gun Turret!

There was a gun turret right on the Cantilever Bridge made of brick and concrete, like a pillbox. They were supposed to put the guns on there if there was an invasion. The home guard would have

Mavis Holt practises wearing her gas mask in her garden at Pearson Avenue, 1940.

manned it. In fact all that happened was that we children went there with our wooden guns and pretended to shoot.

Wendy Wiles

Who Goes There?

They had a soldier on duty on Black Bear Bridge when the raids were on. If you were walking along he'd stop you and say, 'Halt, who goes there?' I used to work the two to ten shift at the 'Alla' [British Aluminium] and I got stopped many a time.

Olive Jackson

Now girls, one little squirt from this stirrup pump will soon put out old Hitler's incendiary bombs! However, soon this works' fire party were taking their job much more seriously.

Stirrup Pumps at the Ready

Every avenue would have its stirrup pump. We had one in our porch with the water bucket and sand for if the avenue needed it.

Wendy Wiles

The Emergency Canteen

During the war I was working on the buses and one day they said to me, 'Put this khaki overall on and go and stand in that bus.' It was a single-decker bus that they'd converted into an emergency canteen for during the blitz. So I stood there inside it, posing with two large tins of Symmington's soup under my arms.

Ada Bate

Time to Play

I remember our school lessons being interrupted by the air raids. I attended Richard Fairclough School and the ruling was that if the parents wished we could run home as soon as the air raid siren sounded and then return as soon as it was over. We quickly forged a number of letters which gave us the opportunity to nip off to Victoria Park for the rest of the day to play football. Our parents were none the wiser and neither were our teachers.

Stan Evans

School in Wartime

We always had to take our gas masks and if you hadn't got your gas mask you had to go home and get it. Then we would get the gas mask out of its case and get a piece of paper and breathe up. If it didn't stick to your gas mask there was something the matter with it and it was taken somewhere to get fixed. There were shelters in the school playground, not that we ever went into them. There was a nursery school as well because the mothers started to go out to work. We stitched pinafores in class for the children to wear while they were in the nursery.

I can remember the Americans coming to visit the school and I had to learn American songs. 'Over There' we had to learn and 'The Star Spangled Banner'. We gave them a song recital when they came. I also used to go round collecting for the Red Cross. I used to go round to the houses near to where I lived and that was instigated by the school.

Freda Ford

Burtonwood in Wartime

When the GIs came here Burtonwood Road was still called Cow Lane because the farmers walked their cattle from the fields and back to the farms. Mr Fryers and his sons had farms there. Cow Lane got changed to Burtonwood Road because it looked and sounded better on the GIs' post.

During an air raid the Germans once bombed Cow Lane, mistaking it for the runway [of the base]. Now Mr Fryers would never go and get proper shelter, he would sleep in bed. When they dropped their bombs one fell right in the middle of his farmyard and blew him out of bed. When he got up he put his foot in the 'guzunder' [chamber pot]. We all had a good laugh and after that he always went in the cellars under the farm during the air raids!

Until the base was built, Burtonwood was farms and mining only. Later, people were

Ada Bate poses with a tin of Symington's soup inside Warrington's new emergency canteen.

The commander of the US airbase at Burtonwood presents the American flag to the Mayor of Warrington in 1945 as a symbol of friendship.

employed to work on the base. Some farmers kept more pigs because they could obtain and collect swill from the camp mess houses and there was plenty to go round. We had to walk over the farmers' fields collecting shrapnel which had fallen when the anti-aircraft guns around had been firing during an air raid. Some of the shrapnel was large and could break farm equipment so us young lads got a few pennies for doing the rounds.

John Leslie Hearn

Twopennyworth of Fades

Food was in very short supply and one of the highlights of the week was to call in Waterworth's fruit shop in Bridge Street and ask if they had twopennyworth of 'fades'.

Usually this was a large box of slightly damaged fruit which would last until the following Saturday. We couldn't buy sweets and chocolate and I can remember sitting in a group with the rest of the lads chewing candle wax like chewing gum. Almost all my class would buy raw carrots to take to school to chew as toffees.

Stan Evans

Chicken Feed

As food was so strictly rationed in wartime my mother decided to keep chickens because we had quite a large garden. She got some day-old chicks from a local farmer and reared them round a light bulb in a box in the spare bedroom. She had some White

Leghorns and some Rhode Island Reds, which were her favourites. She made the mistake of giving them all names and the white cockerel got known as Cheeky because he dipped his beak in a can of green paint once. He was obviously the ring leader and had quite a few adventures, even falling into the air raid shelter once and getting trapped in there for a few days.

My mother was very fond of that bird but our neighbour wasn't because Cheeky would attack anyone apart from my mother. One day he couldn't stand it any longer and told her that Cheeky had been stealing his own chickens' feed. Everyday the cock waited until feeding time next door and then flew over the fence, followed by more of his flock, and pushed all the neighbour's chickens out of the way while he tucked in. When he was challenged he flew into the neighbour's face squawking loudly and the neighbour beat a hasty retreat. As even chicken scraps were too valuable to waste, my mother promised to keep Cheeky in order in future.

Like all her brood Cheeky eventually met his fate but as my mother could never bring herself to eat her pet my grandfather, who wasn't so squeamish, ate him and said he was very tasty!

Janice Hayes

Down on the Farm

I had to do war work in the Second World War and I went to work on Rowswood Farm, the home farm at Walton, with another girl. I worked all the war years there but I didn't actually go into the Land Army because we only lived at Hatton, so we were living at home. I did everything, including horse driving, and I remember one horse called Boxer. He was a devil that horse, and it knew when we were driving it and not the chap that usually drove it, and it played tricks on us. It knew we were frightened of it really I think. They used to put me on its back and send me off to the smithy at Daresbury to get it shod. I daren't get off because it wouldn't stand still while I got on it again! One time those Bowaters' wagons used to be coming down the road with the sheets all flapping and one time it went past us. Boxer reared up in the air, kicking its back legs up, and here I was sticking up there like grim death!

We had some grand times really but we used to have to work hard. Six o'clock in the morning we'd be getting the potatoes and we'd be working till eleven at night in the

Elizabeth Hayes with her hand-reared Rhode Island Red hens.

corn. We used to have to put it all up in stooks, there were no combine harvesters then. We used to work on the threshing machines too.

May Green

Make Do and Mend

I had my children during the war and everything was very tight and your clothing coupons didn't go very far. You'd try to buy some clothing coupons off someone or swap. Say they used a lot of sugar, you'd swap the sugar for say half a dozen clothing coupons. Me and my next door neighbour did a lot of swapping because we never had enough tea and she never had enough washing powder. That's the only way we survived and nobody really realized how hard it was.

It was make do and mend with everything. I've unravelled many a jumper and knit it up again several times. I remember making my son a little jacket, a pair of trousers and a school cap out of my father's old overcoat. I unpicked it, washed the pieces, turned it and put the faded pieces inside. You turned the turn-ups on trousers and you turned the collars on shirts if they got frayed.

We were all in the same position; none of us had much money and we had to queue for everything. I've walked all the way to town with three babies in a pram to the shop in Market Street that sold savoury ducks. I bought a quarter of brawn to go on their dad's sandwiches to take to work the following day. I walked all that way and I was living at Paddington at the time.

Brawn was one of the odd things that wasn't on ration. Corned beef was rationed and liver and stuff like that. You were in

luck if you got a kidney occasionally. I've queued up for hours for two tomatoes – and with three children.

Vera, Laira Court Memories Group

The Westy Landmine

Growing up in Warrington in the early 1950s I often listened to my parents reminiscing about their life during the Second World War. They often told me the story of what happened the night their house was damaged in an air raid. At the time we lived in Mersey Walk at Westy but my parents attended Padgate Methodist Chapel on the other side of the town.

One night the air raid siren went when they were at Padgate and it was such a bad raid that they decided that it wasn't safe to go home and stayed the night with relatives. They didn't get much sleep because of the anti-aircraft fire and so were making a cup of tea in the kitchen early the next morning when their host's young lodger, a policeman, came in from his night shift. Not knowing where my parents lived he sought to reassure them by saying that there wasn't much damage at Padgate. Kingsway and houses across the Mersey had got the worst of it he said. There was instant panic and my parents set off home on foot as fast as they could.

As they walked down Kingsway they saw a pair of houses with their windows blown out. Even more anxious now they hurried over Kingsway Bridge, down Bridgewater Avenue and into Brook Avenue. They noticed that some houses were completely intact and yet those next door had a lot of damage. They learned later that the damage was caused by the rippling shock waves from

Blast damage caused by the Westy landmine.

a landmine.

As they got near the end of Brook Avenue my mum noticed an upturned bowler hat rolling forlornly in the gutter – and it looked faintly familiar. Sure enough, when my father picked it up there were his initials on the hatband. If the hat had been blown that far, what would the house be like? Picking their way over broken glass they walked on.

As they turned the corner a sad sight met their eyes. Our house and our neighbours' had no windows and our front door had been blown clean off its hinges and was jammed over the knob at the bottom of the stairs. At least that had kept any potential looters out and even my parents had a struggle to get in. Gingerly my mother opened the living room door to discover glass fragments and a thick coating of soot from the chimney all over the carpet and furniture.

Their bedroom looked quite untouched at first glance. My mother's best gold eider down still lay neatly on the bed, much to her relief because she was very proud of it. Then she noticed that it seemed strangely lumpy while the room seemed unusually draughty. Looking up she realized that the plasterboard ceiling was no longer in place. In fact the pieces of it were now tucked snugly under the eider down! That had been lifted up by the force of the blast and sucked sideways while the plaster fell onto the bed and then the cover had floated down again over the rubble.

My father and our next door neighbour, Bill Bridge, were both air raid wardens and so as they went out to help with the damage around the area my mother and Mrs Bridge set about packing up their furniture and belongings. These were taken away for storage in the old Malt Kiln in Bank Street whilst the houses were repaired. Just before

Bill Bridge left his house he decided he needed a bath because he was filthy from handling the rubble. As he emerged clean again from the bath he discovered that every stitch of clean clothing had already gone off in a drawer to the Malt Kiln.

When I came to work as a teacher at the Museum in Warrington I always used to tell this story to the children who had come to study wartime Warrington because it helped to make the war seem more real. Then two odd things happened. First I discovered that the museum actually had in its collection a piece of the parachute cord of the very land mine that had fallen that night. Then more recently I was looking through some wartime photographs, which had just been donated, showing police records of the raid at Westy. Sure enough there were the two houses my parents had described on Kingsway and another picture of a house with its windows blown out which I am sure was our house!

Janice Hayes

The Thames Board Bomb

The plane was so low that you could see the pilot. We were playing cricket off Lousher's Lane and pretended to shoot him down with the cricket bat, as children do.

Wendy Wiles

Crrrrump!

I remember the bomb dropping on Thames Board. My father and I were walking over Lousher's Lane and if he'd have opened up on us with his guns he'd have wiped us out.

The next minute there was a sound like 'Crrrrump' as the bomb exploded.

Bob Smith

A Tremendous Bang

I remember on Saturday afternoon as a young teenager being in the Ritz Cinema [later Mr Smith's nightclub]. Suddenly there was a loud tremendous bang and the whole cinema shuddered as if in an earthquake. It was frightening and nobody appeared to settle down to enjoy the film after that.

Little did we realize how close to death we had been until we discovered that a German pilot had circled the Wilderspool football ground where they were playing a home match. He had then dropped his bombs on the Thames Board playing fields where they were holding a family sports day and gala. Several people were killed. It was reported that the plane was shot down near the coast.

Stan Evans

Life Inside the Burtonwood Base

Mr and Mrs Eastwood lived at the small lodge at Bewsey Bridge and on the right of this was the road to Bewsey New Hall. Across from the Hall was Bewsey New Hall Gardens where we lived. There was a five-barred wooden gate there to keep the cattle and horses inside the fields. When the camp was made, the entrance was at this gate and the guardroom was there. The Air Police and later the American Military Police were on duty there to check passes. As we lived inside the base we all had to

Bruce, a GI from Burtonwood base, and Eric Hearn.

have passes and the people who visited us.

When the camps were made, Site 4 was through the gateway near Eastwoods' Cottage, then there was the large PX Stores (where Gulliver's World was later sited) and next was Camp 5. The camps were all around us and the road went on right to Mary Anne Site and the main base. It was late at night when the GIs moved in and it woke us up. There were planes going over and lights and noise as the men moved into the billets on the camps.

When the German planes were trying to find the BRD and the air base they would drop flares to try and light the area up. My father said that for safety he would make us up some bunks inside the wine cellar at Bewsey New Hall, section this part off with a door and put oil lamps and an oil stove in to keep it warm during the air raids. He put whitewashed rings around the trees so that we could find our way home.

I had the freedom of the camps, talking to the GIs in their billets and going to the PX, which was across from us. Entertainment was very good. There were films, live shows, boxing, wrestling and dancing. Girls from Bewsey and the town were allowed on the bases for dancing. Film stars and entertainers visited the troops as well as dance bands. I was always allowed in with a pass which was given to me and also my brothers.

At the rear of New Hall Gardens,

A permit for entrance to the Burtonwood base.

through the trees you could see into Site 5 or walk in the woods around and along the stream by the site. Near the main gate at that end of Site 5 they had a round grass plot with a flagpole in the middle and a cannon at one side. My brothers and I watched a few times at about five past or ten past seven in the evening when the cannon was sounded off to bring down the Stars and Stripes flag. All the GIs would be walking down the long main road from the main base to the camps after their working shift and you could set your watch by it as the siren would sound for an air raid. Well the GIs just scattered to the air raid shelters and as you looked up in the sky you could see black dots which were planes flying over. It was double summertime then and it could keep light until midnight.

The GIs from 4 and 5 sites used to play baseball on Bewsey School playing field near The Towers, which was one of the large houses down Lodge Lane. Boys and girls played around Mrs Eastwood's lodge waiting for the GIs going to town for a night out. They asked them, 'Have you got any gum, chum?' and the GIs gave them some. I liked their dentine and blackjack gums.

We got to know the GIs from the camps. They came round and called dad 'Pop', and loved to hear him talk about the history of Bewsey Old Hall and Bewsey New Hall. One of the GIs we got to know was Irvine D. Hemel and after the war my eldest brother Eric went to live in the States and started a store in Cliftonville, Ohio, in TV and radio with Irvine as his partner.

Towards the end of the war the family decided to move to the USA and start a new life. We sold up ready for moving, had our medicals and were sworn in at the American Consulate, but the property we wanted and a farm fell through and we never did move over there. Eric stayed in the USA with his family and when my sister-in-law came over here for a visit in 1996 she could not find where Site 5 was because of the roads and houses that had been built there.

John Leslie Hearn

Chuck's Club

I remember Chuck's Club. Charles Santarone – but they used to call him Chuck – from the Burtonwood base built a club for the kids at the back of what's now Woolacombe Close. It was built strictly out of the wooden packing cases they brought the planes in to Burtonwood.

Bob Smith

Santarone's Youth Club

Charles Santarone, or Chuck, was an American and he was very friendly with a girl from Secker Avenue, Ada Malpas. Ada had a brother named Reginald and one day Reg was playing football in the street with a few of the lads. The football was made up of newspapers tied up with string because the neighbours didn't like us to play with a leather football as it damaged the plants if it went into their gardens – which you couldn't help at times. Chuck came to join us kicking this pile of newspapers about. He inquired, didn't we have a club or a football pitch where we could play with a decent ball? The answer of course was, 'No money and no materials.'

I believe it was Ada that approached some of the neighbours and asked them to get together to suggest where we could play football. She also said that Chuck would approach his colonel to see if he could supply the materials. Sure enough the colonel okayed all this.

A committee was formed and what we had to do then was find a site. There were

A concert party at Santarone's Club in 1946.

three places suggested. The first was the Sand Pit, the second was J. Richardson's field where the horses used to rest after delivering the coal. The third one was what we called 'The Bottom Field' and I believe this belonged to the Manchester Ship Canal Company. The first two sites were refused but permission was granted for the third, which was later to become Woolacombe Close. Anyway these plans for the club were done and passed by the Borough Surveyors at Warrington.

We approached Chuck and said that we had the field and could he start supplying the materials? This was soon done and the Americans started delivering all these packing crates which were being brought from America with the B42 bombers. Wasn't they large and heavy! Too heavy for the likes of us to lift off these low-loaders, which were supplied by the American base, so they even brought their own lift. This lifted the crates off the low-loaders, over the bottom railway line and onto the field.

Well, we started to strip the crates down, saving all this good timber, which was all tongue and groove and beautiful spars. There was hundreds and hundreds of nails – they must have gone berserk! We even kept the nails and straightened what we could and these were used in the club. We had sacks of them.

The club was completed and the name of the Santarone Youth Club was born. The American colonel who supplied the materials came to visit on the day it was opened and cut the ribbon. Tea, cakes and sandwiches were supplied by most of the neighbours. Stuff was still hard to get because things were still on ration but the Yanks chipped in again for sugar, butter etc.

A second large hut was built and this was to house most of the tools which were again given by the Americans. These tools were to instruct the boys on craft and joinery and also to keep the club maintained.

The club was open six days a week but closed on Sundays. Saturday night was dance night and Monday night was dance lessons taught by Mr and Mrs Inglefield on modern dancing, the waltz, the quickstep and the tango. We had some good nights there and some good times. There was whist drives, we played dominoes, we played darts and we had bagatelle. We had lots of things we wouldn't have had if Chuck hadn't have supplied this building material.

I remember in 1946-7, they used to hold these special dances on a Saturday night. Of course this was in summer because, as there was no electricity, everything had to be by candle at night-time or by hurricane lamp. These special dances went with a swing and the proceeds from these dances were sent to the members serving in HM forces. I remember receiving £2.50 in a postal order and it was in a registered envelope. I was truly grateful for this at the time because £2.50 was four weeks' money to me when I was in the forces. I don't know what they charged the members for those dances but it must have taken a lot of Saturday nights to make up the money that they sent us. It was very nice of them, they didn't forget the members, and that's what I liked about it.

The Santarone Youth Club flourished for a number of years and for me it has great memories. After serving two years abroad I was disappointed to see the club closed. People just lost interest, there were broken windows and smashed doors; it was a shame really. In 1950 I left Secker

A wartime Christmas party for local children organized at Burtonwood American Air Base. As a special treat the children were given scarce oranges!

Avenue and the Loushers Lane estate so I don't know what happened to it after that. I believe most of the wood was sent to the Warrington Rugby Union Football ground, which was at the top of Loushers Lane, to make good their club.

Tom Harris

Oranges Off Ration!

The crews of the Liberty Boats coming along the Manchester Ship Canal used to throw over things to us. The first Liberty Boat that came over from America hadn't realized about the Cantilever Bridge. They went sailing merrily along and its masts

broke! So then they had to have the masts so they could bend down when they went under the Cantilever. The Liberty ships were very like buckets, they were very broad so when they were coming up the canal they just had to lean out to give you your orange or whatever.

Wendy Wiles

Meeting James Stewart

During the last war I worked at Burtonwood Air Base where I remember meeting Jimmy Cagney, Bob Hope and Glenn Miller. One day I was introduced to this pilot who wore a leather jacket with a

St Stephen's Street celebrates the end of the war in Europe with a VE Day party in 1945.

white silk scarf. He was James Stewart the film star. I made some good friends at Burtonwood. After the war I went to America to visit them and I have been writing to one of them for over fifty years.

Vera Foster

Over Paid, Over Sexed and Over Here!

I well remember the GI invasion in the Second World War and again post-war and visiting Burtonwood Air Base. They were so generous with parties for the children. Later of course many married Warrington girls and my mother's two sisters, who were only three and five years older than I was, became GI brides. I remember the excitement in the air because these Americans represented Hollywood and a

better way of life, a richer life than we'd been used to. Although one of their marriages ended in divorce, the other lasted until her husband's death. As travel became cheaper they visited Warrington and we visited them.

I seem to remember that during the American 'occupation' people used to say cynically that the only virgins left in Warrington were the four angels on top of the Town Hall Gates!

Audrey Lewis

Celebrating the End of Rationing

Joe Arrowsmith from Slater Street in Latchford had a baker's business and he used to come to the door with trays of cakes, bread and sausage rolls. When the war ended I bought twelve chocolate eclairs and I ate them all myself! We hadn't been able to get them you see because of the rationing.

Dorothy Kennedy

A VE Day Bonfire

We had a whacking great party and we set Mrs Betley's house on fire! We had a party in Pearson and Westbrook Avenue. The mums had obviously saved the rations and we had jam sandwiches and spam. Everybody had put the flags out. We put the bonfire on the grass in front of Mrs Betley's house and Mrs Parkin's house. The sparks went from the fire on to Mrs Betley's Union Jack which was poking through the window. The next thing was the curtains were going up. We heard language we'd never heard before!

When the bonfire started going down it was quite dark and there weren't any street lights. We crept up the avenue and swiped one of the neighbour's gates because it was all wood. Then we ran back and shoved that on the bonfire!

Wendy Wiles

Burtonwood in 1948

I went to work at Burtonwood Base as a shorthand typist in 1948 when I was nineteen years old. I was paid by the Air Ministry and I was cleared up to Secret Level. I worked for what they called Area Activities, typing for the six officers who used to go out for about a week at a time doing reports on the different areas.

When I first went there the fencing and

Mavis Holt at work as shorthand typist at the Burtonwood Base in 1948.

Mavis Holt and her workmates pose with a GI at Burtonwood one lunchtime in 1948.

everything was all broken down and when we went in each morning we'd see all these girls getting washed in the toilets because they'd been on the base all night. Then I saw the fencing built up again after six months and they couldn't get in any more. I remember them talking about a woman who'd dressed up as a GI and lived on the base.

There were hundreds of GIs on the base and when I'd been there for a couple of years the coloured GIs came. The other GIs weren't going to have this and said they wouldn't eat in the same dining room. They had to accept it and we had one coloured sergeant who worked with us and everything was all right. They were all in the forces and they were all doing the same job so I think they accepted it within the forces.

On the fourth of July they had stalls and a fairground on the base and they always made a big fuss on that day. There was a lot of entertainment on the base. I saw Bob Hope, Billy Graham the evangelist and Danny Kaye. In Warrington we were never short of anywhere to go. We had the naval camp at Stretton, Padgate Camp and Burtonwood – yet I finished up marrying someone from the same avenue!

Mavis Holt

CHAPTER 9

Special Days

Celebrating King George V's Silver Jubilee at Oakwood School in 1935.

Christmas in the 1920s

Hodgkinson's in town always had a Father Christmas. Hodgkinson's was *the* shop and I don't remember one in any other shop. We decorated the room with a holly bush. My father was a joiner so he made a wooden frame so we could tie little bits of holly on so we got a nice shape. We called it a Christmas tree and hung bright things on it, little tins of sweets, toffee things and little sugar mice. Quite a few of them had little numbers on and we had games and then you picked a number and chose your prize. It looked beautiful and it didn't make a mess like a tree.

Phyllis Pickering

Christmas Only Lasted Two Days

We used to make our own decorations. We used to cuts strips of crêpe paper and make chains. We used to make lanterns out of a triangular piece of paper by folding it and cutting slots down the centre of it. Then we would stick it together using a paste made out of flour and water. I don't remember having a Christmas tree but we used to get pieces of holly and hang them together to make a bush.

Christmas presents depended whether you were well off or not and there were four of us so we didn't get a lot. It was a case of an apple, an orange and a few nuts. They wouldn't give individual presents but get a big tin of toffees or some games between us all. We all had a little present from our mum. Probably my brothers would get Meccano or train sets and I would get those embroidery boards with a picture on and you had to do the embroidery through it. You might get

Solitaire with the beads or some knitting that my mother had made up and put in a fancy bag with some wool. Then I'd go round to my well-off friends and they would have dolls and prams, but there was only one child in the family.

We always had Christmas dinner with all the trimmings and a Christmas pudding with a threepenny bit in it. Then we all sat round the table and listened to the King's speech on the wireless. After a nice Christmas tea we put a plank across two chairs to make a stage and we all got up and sang our party piece – a bit of poetry or somebody sang a song. Then we all sang carols around the fire. Christmas lasted just two days then before everybody went back to work.

Margaret Barlow

A Warrington fireman prepares to play Santa to local children in the 1940s.

Celebrating Christmas at Warrington Infirmary around 1940. Many of these children would still have found the Christmas tree a novelty.

Christmas in the 1940s

I was the youngest of five so it was very busy at home. I remember we used to have a kissing bush which we used to decorate with little things. I don't remember a Christmas tree when I was young but later on we did have one. We also had mistletoe and paper chains that you could buy that went up like a concertina.

My mother was always baking. I can remember her making Christmas puddings; I can see the basins now. She used to wrap them in muslin and steam them in the boiler that she used to do the washing in. On Christmas Day I remember the pillowcase at the end of the bed with fruit in, an apple and an orange. I remember once we got a pomegranate, which was unusual. For Christmas dinner we had chicken, which was a rarity.

I remember one year we went to one of

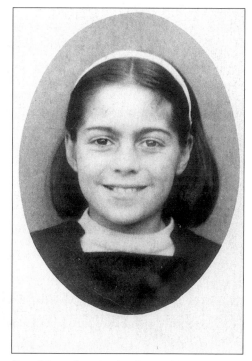

Betty Hayes (later Stephens) in 1950.

my mother's sisters, my Aunt Elsie and her husband used to play the accordion and we'd sing. You'd make your own entertainment that way before TV. Later we used to go to a pantomime in Warrington at the Royal Court Theatre. I remember going right to the Gods and sitting on a wooden bench, a semi-circular wooden bench. I used to think it was marvellous if you were on the front row because you could lean over the rail. Christmas was very short, just two days really.

Betty Stephens

Christmas Was Always Special

Mam would save up for months at the local newsagents and just prior to Christmas she would take delivery of a selection box that would make our mouths water. This would also be accompanied by the current comic annual. I received my main present on Christmas Eve when Mam and Dad went off to the Labour Club. For years it was a mouth organ that I used to play. A large chicken was plunged into a zinc bath and plucked bald. I can still remember the obnoxious smell but that did not put us off the meal on Christmas Day. It was probably the one occasion when we all sat down together. In the evening neighbours were invited in and a good time was had by all.

Ray Brookes

New Year's Eve Celebrations

Market Gate was so narrow you could almost shake hands across it. There used to

Getting ready for the Christmas party at Oakwood Infants' School in the 1940s or 1950s.

A fine display of Christmas poultry at Bowcock's stall in the old Warrington Market in the days when chicken was a treat for Christmas dinner.

Stan Smith, aged seven, eating a hot cross bun at a time when Easter was still not commercialized.

be a policeman stood in the middle on point duty. Every New Year's Eve I think every Warringtonian used to go to Market Gate. There were thousands there. They'd come out of the dances at twelve o'clock and be dancing with a policeman!

Mrs Bradley

Easter Eggs

Just before Easter time when I was seven years old the photographer for the *Warrington Guardian*, who lived across the road, took a picture of me with a box of hot cross buns and a bottle. I was dressed in my school cap, overcoat and scarf and I was sitting on a stool eating a hot cross bun.

This picture was printed in the *Guardian* as an advert for Easter hot cross buns. In those days people didn't go for the chocolate Easter eggs as they do today. At the time I thought I was big to have my picture in the paper.

Stan Smith

The Girls' Maypole

The first of May would see lots of kids dressed for the maypole and this was a good way of getting some money out of folks. The maypole was a decorated pole with a bell and long tapes which were fastened at the top for the 'maypolers' to hold. Each person, usually girls, would dress up as a character. The traditional characters were a queen, a fairy, a flower girl, a rose girl, Miss Muppet, a gypsy and Britannia. There was also the pole holder and two collectors who would go round and collect the money after they had knocked on all the doors to tell everyone that the maypole was outside. The maypole began with everyone dancing round the pole holding a tape and singing:

> 'Here we come gathering nuts in May,
> Nuts in May, nuts in May,
> Here we come gathering nuts in May,
> To crown our Fairy Queen.'

The queen would then sing:

Market Gate before the widening of Horsemarket Street in the mid-1930s.

Thelwall maypole dancers celebrate the Coronation of King George V in 22 June 1911.

'Who crowns me, who crowns me
Who crowns me Queen of the May?'

The fairy would wave her wand over the queen's head and sing:

'I crown you, I crown you,
I crown you Queen of the May.'

The flower girl would then perform her dance on the spot singing:

'I'm the Flower Girl, the pretty Flower Girl,
I'm the prettiest Flower Girl you ever saw.'

Everyone would then dance around the pole singing 'She's the Flower Girl' … and so on. Then came the turn of the gypsy who would sing whilst dancing on the spot:

'I'm a merry Gypsy Jane,
In yon town and in yon lane,
Selling baskets full of pegs,

And a fortune told as true.
So where I go, you all should know,
I'm a merry Gypsy Jane.'

Then everyone sang: 'She's a merry Gypsy Jane' and so on. Britannia would then sing her song and then the maypolers would sing, 'Rule, Britannia'. So it went on with each person singing a song relating to their character followed by the whole group echoing each song.

Lillian Whitfield

The Boys' Maypole

May the 1st, or May Day, was heralded in by maypole dancing. The girls all wore fancy dress and paraded round our immediate neighbourhood performing this maypole ritual with characters like Gypsy Maid, Fairy Queen and Little Bo Peep.

Maypole dancers in Archer Avenue, Latchford, in 1947.

They all sang their respective solos in turn, with an occasional chorus.

The lads' maypole was a burlesque of the girls'. We too would dress up by wearing old clothes or by turning our jackets inside out and blacking our faces. We sang traditional maypole ditties, very much in a nonsensical manner, with words that had no sense or reason. One song went like this:

> 'Underneath the mountain,
> Underneath the ground,
> Where chipped potatoes
> Cannot be found.
> Listen to the elephants
> Singing in the trees.
> Eye tiddily eye tye
> Joe Plum.'

We too performed our little charade and we collected coppers as we went, as did the girls. I suppose we were really begging for money, but everybody enjoyed it and it certainly brightened up the neighbourhood. We were all a little sadder when May Day had gone.

Ernie Day

May Day Horse Parades

I can see those horses now! They will be forever a part of my childhood; a magic that is no more. I believe that it was in 1901 that a group of local businessmen reintroduced the May Horse Parade and they became an annual event which all the townspeople looked forward to. The horses were judged not only on cleanliness and general grooming but also on the correctness of their harnesses, the fit of collars, chains and straps. A number of trophies were awarded and the competition was fierce. I heard that on the night before the parade it was quite common for the drivers to sleep in the stables so as to be ready at first light to start the long process of grooming.

The parades had stopped because of the First World War and they weren't revived again until 1930. At the time I was five years old and we lived in a small terraced house near to the town end of Knutsford Road. Happily, Victoria Park had been chosen as the venue that year and I was able to watch the horses going up on one side of the road to the parade ring, then see them coming back down the other side, proudly wearing their rosettes.

I well remember the heavy draught horses belonging to the railway and canal companies. Their massive hooves clanged

The runner-up in a local horse show poses proudly in Knutsford Road in 1912.

and slipped on the stone sets with which the roads were then surfaced. Then there were the teams of matching thoroughbreds, the pride of the breweries. Looking almost dapper in comparison were the elegant horses with black satin coats used by Lowden-Wells, the funeral director.

I must confess that I had a soft spot for the hawkers. Tinkers, rag-and-bone men, they might have been, but on the day of the parade their ponies stood with fluttering ribbons and jingling harnesses to be judged alongside some of the best horseflesh in the district.

Dolly! That was her name. She was the milkman's horse and 10,000 demons wouldn't have got that animal past our house in a morning until mother or myself had given her that customary crust.

Later on, equestrian sports and a dog show was added to the May Horse Parade

and during the later 1930s it took place on the Rugby Union Football field in Loushers Lane. The show started again after the last war and since then it's become a popular Spring Bank Holiday attraction. Yet I keep remembering that parade of 1930. I can hear the ring of iron on stone and see a rich chestnut mane lifting in the May breeze. To this day I miss Dolly. After all you can't give a crust of bread to an electric milk float, can you?

Joan Hornby

Walking Day

When I was young I'd have my new little pair of short pants, new socks and sandals – Jesus sandals – a white shirt, a blazer and a little collar and tie. That was all bought

117

Friars Green Sunday School in Buttermarket Street in a 1950s Walking Day parade.

specially for Walking Day and then it was your Sunday best. I'd always have a rose out of the garden too.

I remember the Ragged School used to have a great big net that stretched from one side of Bridge Street to the other and everybody threw pennies in it. We got a Walking Day penny too and then it went from a penny to threepence. You went to the fair with that. If you had a big family you used to see how much the others had got. Your mother would say, 'How much have you got? Well, give him some.' And you'd say, 'Oh no, I've collected all that!'

Tom Harris

Walking Day in the 1930s

Many a child had the only new clothes they got in a year for Walking Day. I knew that it was Walking Day when I had my new cap and my belt with a snake's motif buckle, together with a new pair of 'gollies', or black galoshes.

For weeks before the event, each church and chapel put hours of work into their theme for that particular year. The Catholic contingencies had all their children dressed in identical outfits in the same colour and style. They were usually linked together as they walked by gaily coloured ribbons. Most of the churches had a brass band to lead them, followed by huge banners depicting the life of Our Lord. These were carried by a sturdy man holding each pole with guy ropes leading out to other youths. The banner carrier had a belted shoulder harness with a cup to receive the butt of the pole and enable him to grasp the pole with both hands. There was often a relief man too to each pole. You can imagine the effort required to manipulate this huge sail-like banner round the route of the procession on a windy day.

The children came next with the toddlers first and with probably a dozen or so proud mums wheeling babies in gaily decorated prams. The older children came next followed by the adult members of the church. In my early days there was usually a local trader with a decorated horse and cart full of youngsters too tiny to walk and this brought up the rear of the procession.

The spectators usually took up their positions hours before the procession started, often in the same spot, year after year. The first walkers gathered on the Town Hall at about 8.30 a.m. and the whole procession took about three hours to pass. As the wonderful cavalcade slowly wound round the streets of the town mothers, fathers, aunts, uncles and friends would run out as a loved one or a friend passed by with gifts of pennies for the walkers.

While my brother and I attended Workingmen's Mission we never took part in a Walking Day because the Mission usually organized a day at the seaside or went to a local field for a picnic. It wasn't until I attended Friars Green Mission at the age of about fifteen that I took part in Walking Day, and very enjoyable it was too. The afternoon was usually spent on a field in the country where games and sports were organized and sandwiches, cakes and buns were distributed as well as tea, ice cream and pop. There was a real carnival atmosphere in Warrington on Walking Day.

Ernie Day

Armistice Day, 1918

In 1918 I lived at 59 Orchard Street, just three doors from the Cockhedge factory gates. After the workers had decorated the mill, the public were asked to go along to view the factory. My mother took my younger sister and me along.

We left the house in our red, blue and white trimmed hats and with red, blue and white ribbons in our hair. The queue stretched from the factory gates to the end of Orford Street and round into Crown Street where we joined it. When we neared the gates Mam gave my sister and I a silver threepenny bit to give to the voluntary collection. Mam gave sixpence, known as a tanner. In all we three gave a shilling and in those days a shilling was a small fortune.

Anyway, we were all taken round the mill. It was beautifully decorated and the weaving sheds were absolutely fantastic.

'God Save the King!' proclaims the banner as Foundry Street celebrates.

Garibaldi Street and Priestley Street enjoy their Coronation Party, organized by Mrs McGrath in June 1953.

The only colours were red, white and blue. How wonderful it looked! What a pity we didn't have colour photography in those days.

Mrs Allen

The Death of King George VI

In my last year in the infants [February 1952] we were having musical movements in the hall. The music was coming from a wireless on the window ledge when suddenly it stopped playing and a man's voice said, 'The King is dead.' I'll always remember that, the shock on the teachers' faces.

Pat Lockett

Queen Elizabeth's Coronation

We had a day off school [for the Coronation in 1953]. All the schoolchildren were given a blue glass tumbler inscribed with the Warrington coat of arms and a tin box with a block of Cadbury's chocolate inside. Very few people owned a television set in those days but we had a neighbour who had one and she invited us inside to watch the Coronation. Later in the day we had a street party. Our mums made the sandwiches and cakes and decorated the house with flags.

Betty Stephens

CHAPTER 10

Leisure

Staff at the Star Kinema, Church Street, which opened in January 1914.

Street Entertainers

The local workhouse was at the back of Whitecross Hospital in Aitkin Street, off Priestley Street. We were often entertained by more than an average collection of street artists of all shapes and sizes. These travelling troubadours would spend the night in the workhouse or 'Spike' as it was known to us, spend the day singing in the streets and then tramp on to the next town or village. We also had our regular barrel organ operator, complete with monkey, as well as acrobats, clog dancers and others.

Ernie Day

Entertainments

A man with a hurdy-gurdy used to come round. He had a great big bear which would

The organ grinder and his monkey were typical street entertainers in the early twentieth century.

dance to the music. Another day a man would come with a little monkey and it used to run along the roofs. A man would come round with a little pony and trap, and it was a halfpenny a ride. Just off Winwick Road was Sam Massey's Field, as they used to call it, which faced Cunningham's Brewery. Every year a group of Red Indians would come there in full regalia!

Every year we used to skate on the meadows at the top of Hale Street. That was before any of the houses were built on the Alder Lane estate. The gypsies used to have a horse sale there on Alder Lane each year. They used to have a May Day horse show when all the horses were dressed up and judged for cleanliness and decoration. We had plenty of entertainment!

Mrs Bradley

A crowd of expectant children follow the man with his performing bear down Orford Road, near Steel Street, around 1910.

Cinemas and the Royal Court Theatre

There were about ten cinemas in and around Warrington, with the Royal Court Theatre and the Hippodrome providing live entertainment. The Royal Court Theatre was in Rylands Street but later Lennon's supermarket and Poll Tax House took over the site. It was usually a special treat like a pantomime or a birthday when we were taken there as kids. More than likely though if my dad had won some extra money in a football sweep or on a bet we would all benefit by a special seat in the centre circle. I can still smell the plush velvet seats and see the heavy curtain drapes draw aside as the orchestra struck up with the overture. Between the wars many famous stars visited the Royal Court and Gracie Fields and George Formby played there before they became famous. In later years, just prior to the Second World War, it became a Repertory Company.

Ernie Day

The Desert Song

There were several cinemas in Warrington and although we did not go very often, one thing does stand out in my memory. The Grand Cinema was showing *The Desert Song* and the manager must have been keen on publicity. He engaged a young unemployed man who lived in the next street to us to dress up as The Red Shadow. I can remember him, complete with flowing Arab robes and brown make-up, riding round the town on a

The Royal Court Theatre in Rylands Street in the early 1900s. It was demolished in 1960 for a supermarket, which later became Poll Tax House.

The Grand Cinema near Wilderspool railway crossing in the 1930s.

donkey and carrying a poster advertising the film. This really caused a stir because nothing like it had ever happened before. Each day after he'd finished his stint, he'd walk home in full regalia down our street and the atmosphere was almost unbearable!

David Plinston

The Pivvy and Other Entertainment

I have wonderful memories of the many happy hours spent in that little cinema in Lovely Lane which later operated as a bicycle shop. My mother used to love the romantic films with all the old stars of the silent films. On reflection they were very far from silent because in the old days many of the older generation were unable

to read and it was quite usual for an older person to be accompanied by a younger member of her family. When the dialogue of the film appeared in captions on the screen there was a steady drone of subdued voices reading out the dialogue. More than likely the poor old people were also a little hard of hearing which meant that the readings had to be a little more than a whisper. However, when the 'talkies' arrived this solved that problem and opened up a wonderful new dimension.

At the Pivvy the programme ran for Monday, Tuesday and Wednesday and then changed for Thursday, Friday and Saturday. The Pivvy was a typical local establishment, patronized mainly by the same folk year after year, and gave much relief from the poverty-stricken days of the early 1930s.

One of the characters connected with this old cinema was a chap called Flash Algie. His main purpose in life was to drink, chain smoke and see that the kids who had paid probably two pence or three pence to sit on wooden forms at the front of the cinema didn't crawl along the floor in the darkness, go under the seats and emerge in the more expensive seats at the back. It was always a constant running battle between Flash and the kids, with Flash being at a disadvantage because of his habitual chain smoking. He always gave away his position in the darkness by the glowing fag end and so the kids would watch the telltale glow and easily outmanoeuvre him!

I remember too when the talkies became established, we kids used to listen at the exit doors which were at either side of the screen and follow the progress of the film. To our great delight, and the annoyance of Flash Algie, we would wait until the audience were on the edge of their seats anticipating the murderer's entrance and then give the doors an almighty kick. Before Algie could get us we were away.

Before the talkies the accompaniment to the film was provided by a pianist and at the Pivvy it was a little man by the name of Mr Foden. Believe it or not he used to play away wearing a pair of wellington boots and with a row of fruit, toffees and bottles of beer ranged along the top of the piano. The boots were a necessity because the piano was situated in a shallow pit beneath the screen and the floor of the hall sloped down rather steeply from the

The Queens Cinema in Orford Lane in the 1930s.

rear to the front where the screen was. Now I cannot remember there being any kind of toilet in the building, consequently anyone feeling the need, especially the kids, used to relieve themselves where they were. All the little rivulets joined other little streams and eventually flowed down to Mr Foden's feet! His refreshment on top of the piano was of course consumed with one hand as he kept pace with the film.

Ernie Day

The Premier

There was the Premier Cinema in Latchford and on Saturday lunchtime the kids would flock out of there. The boys were Roy Rogers fans, and Buster Crabbe and Flash Gordon.

Glenys Nichol

Dance Halls

I've been off dancing every night. There was the Blighty Club in Sankey Street. There was the P and K, that was a big dance hall in Owen Street, a fantastic place. Then there was Ryland's Rec., the Patten Hall and the Parr Hall. There was a dance hall over the Grand Cinema at Bridge Foot. The Empire skating rink was also a dance hall. There was the Palatine off Wilderspool Causeway, that was a roller skating rink.

Dancing was the craze in those days and the lads and girls all used to go together. There was the Lancers, they'd swing you off your feet in that! The Parr Hall was used practically every night until two o'clock in the morning. Three or four of us would go

but my dad used to think that I was in bed. My mum would tell him that when he asked and she'd be trembling in case he caught me!

It only cost about a sixpence or half a crown for a long night's dance until two o'clock in the morning. You could walk home and the policeman would ask if you were all right.

Mrs Bradley

Radio Days

I remember that McDermott's radio shop was in one of the streets by the market and they would play the latest model radios to attract the customers. You would quite often see a crowd of twenty to thirty people gathered round the shop doorway listening to 'Music Hall'. They would laugh with the studio audience at comedy acts like Flanagan and Allen, and Nosmo King, who took his name from a railway carriage sign saying No Smoking. Then there was Billy Bennett, who was billed as 'almost a gentleman', and Kenneth and George, the Western Brothers.

David Plinston

Radio and Television

The wireless was very important and I hardly missed episodes of Paul Temple, Dick Barton and Valentine Dyall's *Man in Black* series. One episode of PC 49 where a doll was always left at the scene of a murder stretched my imagination so far that I visibly shook with fear. Sunday lunchtime was always accompanied by *Family*

Favourites followed by Billy Cotton and one of the comedy slots like *Round The Horn* and *Much Binding in the Marsh*. Mam and Dad always tuned into the news.

The first television aerial round here was mounted on a Brindley Avenue chimney stack in 1952. We were more envious than impressed. By the following year there were perhaps ten just in time for the Coronation.

Ray Brookes

Leisure in the late 1930s

War had started and all at once there was work for everyone. The young men were called up, or volunteered for the services and my sister and all her girl friends learned to dance. We couldn't wait to finish our day's work and rush out to one of the many dance halls in the town. Another of our favourite pastimes was going to one of the ten cinemas in the town.

The only day that there was nothing to do was Sunday. Then we went to church and on nice afternoons we would walk around Bank Park and listen to the band. It was like a huge meeting place. In the evening everyone walked down the left-hand side of Bridge Street from Market Gate all the way to Walton Gardens. Then we'd walk back again on the right-hand side. We always wore our Sunday coats and always a hat and gloves. It was like a ritual.

Lillian Whitfield

Enjoying the fresh air at Walton Gardens around 1950.

An early twentieth-century outing to Frodsham Hill with the popular helter-skelter in the background.

MERSEY VIEW, OVERTON HILL, FRODSHAM.

Outings

Frodsham Hill was our Mecca. We went there on Walking Day and then when we started work at the age of fourteen we got bikes and went to Frodsham on them. I've walked to Frodsham many a time; it was just a change of environment.

My mother, Bertha Scott and other housewives around Lancaster Street used to go for a picnic on Crosfields' Rec. – such simple pleasures that they enjoyed and looked forward to. People used to walk more. We used to set off from Bank Quay and on a Sunday evening with my mother and father we'd go right round the waterworks at Appleton. Then we'd go the other way round, past what we called 'Jacob's Ladder', and back home. All we'd have would be greaseproof paper with some cold potatoes from the Sunday dinner. That was our refreshment on the way round.

When you got to the age of sixteen or seventeen there'd be the 'Rabbit Run' for girls. The girls used to wait at Market Gate and Boots. There was one procession right up Chester Road, all the way up Chester Road, all the way past the waterworks and this way on round where Burtonwood Camp was. You'd just take them for a walk and it was a chance to meet the girls.

Ernie Day